Preston
Tucker
& Others

Tales of brilliant
automotive
innovators &
innovations

T0386796

Also from Veloce –

WWW.VELOCE.CO.UK

First published in February 2011 by Veloce Publishing Limited, Veloce House, Parkway Farm Business Park, Middle Farm Way, Poundbury, Dorchester, Dorset, DT1 3AR, England.
Fax 01305 250479/e-mail info@veloce.co.uk/web www.veloce.co.uk or www.velocebooks.com.

ISBN: 978-1-845840-17-4 UPC: 6-36847-04017-8

Preston
Tucker
& Others

**Tales of brilliant
automotive
innovators &
innovations**

VELOCE PUBLISHING
THE PUBLISHER OF FINE AUTOMOTIVE BOOKS

CONTENTS

INTRODUCTION

This book examines the history of the car from a completely different angle. Forget about the all-powerful, yet rather boring car manufacturers for a moment. Can you imagine a world where everyone drove beautiful, unusual cars, created by talented designers?

Although the car is a technological and rational invention, it is the dreamers and eccentrics who have made the biggest contribution to the development of the automotive industry – those who have had the ability to think beyond their own time and space. Do not believe people who claim that money rules the car business – it is a passion for speed and obsession with mechanics that have driven its progress. Yet, for many a dreamer, this is a passion which has ended in disaster. Misunderstood and pushed aside by their contemporaries, they have been forced to watch their dream get crushed under the feet of the ignorant.

However, we should not call these people the losers. If everyone was afraid to step into the unknown, we would probably still be sitting in caves and painting deer on the damp, bleak walls. A desire to constantly push the boundaries has led us to the technological developments we enjoy today. How many people have been trampled on during this crazy race towards the horizon? We cannot possibly count them all, yet the horizon is where it always was, elusive and deceptive, and we keep on moving to reach it. Hard as we try, we never really get any closer. What else do we expect? There will always be new things to invent, or opportunities to improve the efforts of our predecessors.

Progress is endless. Although the taste of failure is bitter, a man who has followed his dream always leaves something of value behind him. Even if his invention has perished, he will have succeeded in changing the way people think. As we will learn from the fate of this book's heroes, many inventors and trailblazers have been a bit too enthusiastic, and the road to fulfilling their dream has quite often led them into obsession. However, let us not judge them too harshly – the world would be duller and emptier without them. Their dreams and passions have been behind many of the most important, historical technological advances, including those in the car industry.

Many inventions that we tend to attribute to the contemporary car giants were in fact discovered many years before, and few can remember the names of those overlooked, talented people. Who invented the internal combustion engine? Did he earn a lot of money for this idea, or did he die a poor man, mocked and belittled by others? Who can we thank for the sophisticated ABS – the system that helps our cars to brake more safely? What about car design? Is it fair to say that rich curved body forms have only been made feasible with the progress of 3D computer graphics? Maybe the craftsmen of the past were able to create something far more beautiful, aided only by simple wooden mallets and planishing hammers.

Only a few remember those car sculptors whose work could be shown in the best art galleries of the world, alongside Rodin. Aerodynamic and cosmic designs are not a new concept – similar shapes, perhaps even more courageous, were created by car designers back in the '30s. However, people couldn't identify with their ideas at that time. Is it really the case that everything new is really just the well-forgotten old?

Let's show some respect to the dreamers. Our world wouldn't be quite so exciting without them.

PART ONE

THE DREAMERS

JOHN DELOREAN

Here is the author's imagined version of how events may have played out through the Delorean* saga –

It was a fine, sunny day. Park Avenue snaked like an unruly mountain river through Manhattan, dragging the people and their cares along into the dizzying New York world of sounds and smells.

High above the heated asphalt, on the 43rd floor of a skyscraper, a rather different view opened up. The crush of the street lay somewhere deep in the abyss, and the tall buildings glittered in the lustrous sunbeams like gigantic diamonds. Money reigned supreme.

Air-conditioners buzzed softly, keeping the swelter at a distance. A middle-aged man stood by the window. He gazed at the impressive panorama of New York, but seemingly took no notice of it. A silent film from the past ran in front of his mind's eye. Was this young man from the black and white film really him? Earlier on in his life, he thought that he would be living in hopelessness, but then, thanks to his willpower and unshakeable pride, he achieved heights of success that many people could only dream about.

Still, a part of his memory had remained in this black and white film, and, although John strove to bury his memories as deeply as possible, they surfaced from time to time, usually completely unexpectedly.

"Sir, Roy Clark has arrived." The secretary's flushed face appeared in the half-opened door.

"Ask him in," muttered John, waking up from his daydream.

A rather stout little man with a broad smile on his face appeared in the doorway. "Great office, John! Hats off to you! You're really working up your image. It feels like the headquarters of a global corporation here," enthused the guest as he glanced over each interior detail with the eye of an expert.

"Would you sell Gucci footwear in a Bronxdale Avenue cellar?" John asked.

"I wouldn't," laughed the strange visitor. "Actually, I prefer Lloyd's shoes."

"A reasonable choice, my dear friend. If our plans come true, you will be able to buy Lloyd's and all its stock."

"To tell the truth, I could do it now, but I won't. I have my mind set on something else all together. I tell you, John, this business we spoke about the other day has got me really excited."

"I know how to get my audience carried away," observed John haughtily as he swung round and fixed his eyes on a large photo, which hung on the wall, in an ostentatious silver frame. "How do you like it, Roy?" asked John, pointing at the photo.

"Do you say 'it', speaking about your wife?"

"Stop it, dear friend, she's only a woman. A woman and nothing more."

---

* John Delorean originally used this form of his name, later DeLorean.

"Oh, you old chauvinist!"

"Not at all. I'm the most conservative man you've ever met."

"You don't say so! Tell it to the British government – they will refuse to collaborate with you immediately," laughed Clark.

"Labour is just a temporary thing! I bet that in the coming election, the Conservatives will win. I'm absolutely sure about the British government, I'll squeeze anything I wish from them. Several thousand jobs created in a suburb where people were on the booze until now. DeLorean is the magic wand for Northern Ireland."

"Do you think that Irish drunkards would be the best contingent to work with the supercar?"

"Don't dramatise, Roy – their task will be very simple."

Roy frowned; this meant that he had a doubt in his mind. John perceived his friend's mood and was willing to turn their conversation in another direction, when Betty, with her fascinating charm and aromatic coffee, broke the strained silence.

Roy sipped the strong, hot drink slowly, put his cup on the table, and settled down in a comfortable cerise armchair.

"Tell me, John, how do you intend to do it? I'm not a businessman. I have entertained people all my life, but now I want to do other things, too. All that you have told me sounds great, but I must ask a question: How much are you willing to invest in this risky business yourself?"

"Look, Roy, it isn't that simple. We are at the very beginning of our journey and lots of work lies ahead of us. At the moment, I'm looking for answers to many important questions. I've been in this business for a long time – it isn't too difficult to shout at the slow-witted managers of General Motors, but to create a gigantic mechanism from scratch so that it will function perfectly and bring in a great profit, that's quite another matter. You mustn't worry about it, Roy. You won't be the only investor. We have loans, the British government will assign financial resources as you know, and we have several private investors – they are just ardent car lovers like you, Roy. It's only a matter of time until we'll be able to say that our capital is sufficient to begin the real work."

"You are a phrase-monger, John. Which of your speeches is this quote from?" laughed Roy, slapping his knee. "Ain't it just like you? You told me all sorts of fibs, instead of naming the actual sum!"

"I've never complained about lack of success. However, anything could happen in life – this is big business. I've invested a few million in real estate as well ... You know about this mishap with my avocado plantations?"

"Oh, yes, I've heard about it – a bad year. What a pity! I had hoped to get a taste of John DeLorean's home-grown avocados – but it all came to nothing again. Lucky this bad harvest didn't affect Chilean plantations."

"Stop that twaddle, please! You don't like avocados!"

"That's right! I'm just a simple boy from Virginia. Could I ever have imagined, when I first took a guitar into my hands, that I'd earn millions after years of hard work, and end up sitting here haggling with you about investments?"

"Welcome to the world of business sharks!"

Roy straightened up his facial expression. "As far as I understand, you take no part in this enterprise with your own capital."

"If you know of a better man to lead this company, let me know!" John became excited but noticing Roy's troubled gaze, he realized that he was expected to give a straightforward answer. "No, at this moment it seems that I take no part in this deal, but don't worry; everything is fine. If you consent to become our partner, we have sufficient funds, and we're ready to construct the cars at the very moment we get the keys to our new motor plant."

*John Z DeLorean – the man who had the nerve to take on the corporate world.
(Courtesy Cliff Schmucker, Patrick Conlon, with thanks to Josh Haldeman)*

"All right, John, I didn't want to upset you. I will order my lawyer to draw up an agreement – it's very easy to dupe me because we don't know a single thing about the car business in Virginia. Our people live a more simple life – the grass is greener and heaven always seems to be a little closer, but that doesn't mean I don't know the taste of risk. Okay, so be it. Let's build the cars. I can't wait till I get in one and test it myself."

"I guarantee that the second car will be at your disposal. I will crash the first car myself!"

Roy's face lightened after this friendly exchange. He smiled; his doubts all but gone. Whether a country musician or a motor plant investor, everyone wants to try something new. Why not? The dream was just a signature away. Roy left, and John was alone again with his reflections. Was this exaggeratedly large photo of his wife a testimony of his feelings? It was probably only really hanging there to provoke envy in other men he met.

"So beautiful and only half my age! I first saw her on the cover of *Vogue* magazine and I knew at once that she would be my wife."

This was what John had once told his close friend. He liked his friends being envious of him. He sensed it at the evening parties they attended. John's wife looked a million times better than the wives of the other guests. It was magnificent – at moments like that, John felt like king of the world. He recalled the day he proposed to Cristina.

"At last, dear!" exclaimed the beauty when she got an extravagant, sparkling ring.

"Would you marry an unemployed man?" asked John theatrically.

"I would marry a tramp if the tramp was you," answered Cristina, and added, "but why unemployed?"

"I will break the news to you. You have to know before you marry me, Cristina; I have left my job, said good-bye to the awful General Motors, left it forever. I don't want to hear about that company ever again."

"You are a feather-head, but that's the reason why I love you ... You have something up your sleeve, I can feel it. What is it?"

"I wouldn't be me otherwise, would I?" John approached the window and leant on the windowsill. He gazed into the distance and it was obvious that he was daydreaming about the future. It would be dazzling and vibrant. People would admire him and Cristina would be proud of her husband.

"I'll do some work in the Business Communication Association for a year to help people who have been out of work for a long time. It's a charity institution, as you know. I really must step aside from all that car stuff. I can't stand it any more. Sometimes I feel like I hate my Porsche!"

"That's impossible, Johnny, you love it more than you love me," said Cristina impishly.

"Cris, I would push it off a cliff if you asked me to."

"Maybe another time, I wouldn't want to have to go on foot. So, you're saying farewell to cars? Adios and goodbye? The mighty DeLorean, the brilliant car-giant. I'd like to see it."

"You haven't heard all the details yet, my love! When the contract with the Association is over, I'll devote myself to my dream, which has followed me since childhood. I'll construct my own car. Big, beautiful and fast. Such a great car that the old ganders from General Motors could never possibly match it. They couldn't even imagine something like this, it will be a revolution in the motor industry. Everyone who dares to dream will be able to afford DeLorean's supercar. Wait a little while, Cris, and we will have a great life soon."

"I like listening to you," whispered Cristina rapturously. "Don't worry, I have an excellent modelling contract, we won't die of hunger. I will support a family but you can wash the dishes – and don't try to wriggle out of it!"

John knelt in front of Cristina and took her hands. "You are a uniquely beautiful woman. You are like a picture – now you are on my wall, but one fine day you could be on another wall that would be more agreeable for you. But I don't want to think about that – I only wish to enjoy life together with you. Know what? I'll order the biggest frame possible and put your photo into it. I'll hang it on a wall in my office so I can always have you always in front of me."

"I would rather like you to take me down off the wall and take me out to a restaurant," joked Cristina.

"Of course; it's a good job I didn't push my Porsche over a cliff!"

John had had a dream of designing his own car ever since his childhood. This in itself was not too surprising. He was born in Detroit, after all – the automotive capital of the United States. Ask any boy in this town what he wants to be when he grows up and he will answer "… a car engineer!"

John's father worked in the Ford motor plant, and the best of John's memories were connected with that big old works. His father was a rather uneducated and brutal fellow – he boozed every so often and sometimes thrashed his wife and four sons. For all that John would later admit, he had inherited many important character traits from his father. John would bear no hard feelings towards the old tippler though, and would even give his name – Zachary – to his son. But all that was a long way off yet.

John was a very purposeful boy, and he knew early on in his life that he did not want an ordinary and monotonous life like his father. John realised that education was to be the key to his success, and he finished his studies as a car engineer. In 1952, at the age of 27, he took a job in the Chrysler Corporation, but he disliked the company and in one year's time switched from Chrysler to what he regarded as a better prospect – the Packard motor plant.

In the postwar years, Packard was one of the most innovative car producers in the world. Its cars were notable for an extraordinarily curved design and many technical innovations. But as time passed, large American concerns like the Ford Motor Company, General Motors and Chrysler picked up speed and left the independent car producers far behind. John understood that it was the right time to try his luck with any of these automotive giants.

He considered General Motors to be the most progressive company out of the Big Three, and went to apply for a job at a GM branch, Pontiac. The company welcomed the young specialist with open arms, and he was appointed as a director of Pontiac's new technology department. From then on, DeLorean decided to make changing the Pontiac's visual image his main goal. It had to be transformed from a pensioner's car into a cult status symbol for young people. When John arrived at Pontiac, the company's sales volume formed 4 per cent of total US car sales. Mostly thanks to John, within a few years, this figure increased to 6.5 per cent.

The managers were pleased with him, and didn't try to control his progress. They gave him free rein. John, of course, made full use of such an agreeable situation, and

JOHN DELOREAN

in 1963 he began to work on a new, extravagant car. The Pontiac GTO turned out to be a fresh and sporty model. The United States had never seen anything like it before. The local racing enthusiasts previously had no other alternative than to buy an imported Italian or British sportscar – now America had its own supercar, fast and fierce. This was how the 'muscle car' concept was born, and many historians regard the Pontiac GTO as the first ever muscle car.

The commercial manager of Pontiac received instructions to allocate a slot in the production programme of 1964 to 5000 GTO cars. This time, the managers of General Motors had made a blunder. People liked the GTO so much, they had to increase the output very quickly. In the first year, 31,000 GTO cars were sold.

DeLorean triumphed and, of course, a promotion followed. John became the head of the entire Pontiac division, and he began to work like mad. He introduced, in practice, a new management method. He mercilessly fired any worker who, in his opinion, was not in the right place, and he spent big money on new inventions. The drastic methods began to bear fruit, and in just a few years Pontiac evolved into a brilliant enterprise.

The managers of General Motors, noticing how skilfully John managed the division, asked him to take charge of the recovery plans for the unstable Chevrolet division. In just two years, John transformed Chevrolet from a middling producer of mainstream cars into a first-rate car plant. For the first time in the division's history, the annual sales volume amounted to two million cars.

And there you have it. Suddenly, the rational and prudent John found himself completely enamoured with his own success. He grew his hair long and ditched the tedious dark suits. He came to the office dressed in bright shirts and began dating Hollywood starlets and models. Finally, to surprise his boss even more, he dyed his grey hair. During the seventies, a top-class manager with dyed hair was a perfect scandal! At the same time, John accustomed himself to squandering money. General Motors had loads of cash, so the 'purse' often seemed to be bottomless. Need £10,000 for unforeseen expenses or six million dollars to work on a new car? Piece of cake! An application, a few signatures here and there, and a week later, he had the cash at his disposal. Unfortunately, a little later, John would have to understand that money didn't just fall out of thin air in the real world.

In 1972, despite his ambiguous image, John DeLorean became vice-president of General Motors. He moved to the posh GM headquarters, and enjoyed a monthly salary of $55,000. Not that he would have complained about his salary back in Chrysler, but this was better by far.

It was only one more step to the General Motors presidential chair, and everybody was convinced that DeLorean would eventually stand at the helm of the giant enterprise. But the course of events was unforeseeable, and the discord between the ostentatious John and his grey-suited colleagues grew day by day.

In April 1973, John retired from General Motors, having spent only six months in the prestigious post. From then on, he never worked for another employer again.

1975 began, and the work on John's own supercar was in full swing. He had already drawn some excellent drafts, and now the famous Italian car designer Georgetto Giugiaro was helping to give the sketches a more finished look. The Italian had responded favourably to the drawings of the enterprising American, and this had flattered John's ego very nicely. DeLorean had always thought that the most elegant cars were made in Italy.

"I hate all things heavy and clumsy. I am an American, but I don't understand how my fellow people tolerate those road-cruisers. A car should be aggressive yet elegant."

The biggest problem was how to find the funds to produce the new car. John, used to wasting money, couldn't change his extravagant lifestyle even now that the seemingly bottomless purse of General Motors was closed to him forever. Yet he realised that he'd be able to attract rich investors, thanks to his brilliant reputation.

DeLorean, regardless of his dubious retirement from General Motors, was still the golden boy in the eyes of the American business world, and still a great talent known for his high-quality work.

Playing on his reputation, and cleverly networking with the business sharks, DeLorean soon raised the capital needed to build the plant and start production of the car. The guys at General Motors had a good laugh at his efforts – nobody had managed to open and run a successful independent car plant in the United States within the last seventy years.

But John did the right thing – he was far-sighted and confident, as only a man who knows his own strengths can be. At first, he was considering building his new plant in Puerto Rico, but dropped the idea when he read an article about the Ulstermen being overwhelmed by unemployment.

Without delay, he took a plane to see this gloomy place with his own eyes. Northern Ireland welcomed its benefactor with a sky full of steel-grey thunder clouds. The barren plain, where the DeLorean's dream plant would be built, looked repulsive. Nobody could ever imagine that, within a year, one of the most modern motor plants of its time would stand in this damp place, and more than 2000 families would be saved from poverty.

The British Labour government was well disposed towards John. The matter of the contract was settled within quite a short time; moreover, the government assigned a noteworthy grant of £140 million to back the American investor. People who had doubted DeLorean would succeed in building a single car now ceased spreading the rumours, and waited in awe to see what would happen next.

John was flying high on the initial success. He took a suitcase full of drafts and caught a plane to England to meet Colin Chapman. The old engineer, chief of the famous Lotus company, was undoubtedly one of the most respected experts in the industry. It was said that Chapman could construct a car out of hardly anything at all, and, in addition, do it blindfolded. DeLorean had decided to ask Chapman to prepare his dream car for mass production. But Chapman, for an unknown reason, didn't finish the work on this car, even though Lotus received almost 18 million dollars for the job that was never finished. Later, as we will see, somebody would get put behind bars for this.

Meanwhile, John needed to find people who would finish the preparation work. He decided to entrust this important task to his old friends from the General Motors era. They were a team of retired GM engineers who managed to round off this work in just six months. They had to work out all the complicated technological processes of how to construct a car out of a heap of parts and components. The larger car manufacturers need around 18 to 24 months to see a prototype through to a conveyor-ready car, so six months was very impressive indeed.

DeLorean himself undertook the planning of his plant. John had spent his whole life in various motor plants. He knew exactly what was right and what was wrong. Working in the Chevrolet division, he had seen many mistakes allowed by car manufacturers. He put the first brick into the foundation of the motor plant in October 1978 and in late 1980, the first DeLorean DMC-12 rolled out through the gate of the brand-new supermodern factory. The cars made their way to willing buyers who had waited impatiently for the DMC-12.

It seems that during those two years, nobody talked about anything else but John DeLorean's experiment to conquer the summit of the car business. The first six months

The DMC-12 with 'wings' spread. (Courtesy Cliff Schmucker, Patrick Conlon, deloreanproject.com)

Johnny Carson, famous American TV star and one of many celebrity investors, with Cristina and John having fun at the official launching banquet. (Courtesy Cliff Schmucker, Patrick Conlon)

saw 3500 DMC-12s being snapped up by eager customers. John had triumphed – he had given hell to the old muttonheads of General Motors. A former outsider had now become a serious competitor. John was convinced that his DMC-12 could successfully compete with the Chevrolet Corvette and thought that, compared to the aging Corvette, his DMC-12 was just what the '80s needed.

There were a lot of obstacles, though. John had estimated the retail price to stand at $10,500. Nevertheless, when the dealers received the price list, it was scary enough to leave them speechless. The basic price of a DMC-12 was to be $25,000!

"Why is it so expensive?" they asked.

"It is a DeLorean, my friend! People appreciate fine things," answered John.

In the beginning, people eagerly snapped up the cars, mainly because of the unique design – the DMC-12 was the first and only mass production car in the world to have an unpainted body. The stainless steel body panels looked extremely impressive because the light played on the surface in all colours of the rainbow as you drove it along. Only a few knew the truth. Some claim that John's intention was completely different – he planned to paint his cars red, yellow and black; however, the unskilled

*The DeLorean DMC-12 revealed – people had never seen anything like it before.
(Courtesy Cliff Schmucker, Patrick Conlon)*

Irish workers were unable to master the new, complicated methods of painting technology. New evidence speaks against this version. DeLorean's early sketches and notes suggest that he had actually planned to build a stainless steel monster.

The imposing appearance was the trump card of the DMC-12. The European design, coupled with large American dimensions, made the car a worthy competitor. In the eighties, hardly any concept car was as thrilling as the mass-production DeLorean DMC-12. The exceptional gull-wing doors added a special charm to the silver giant.

DeLorean constructed his car to suit his own height. Even a basketball player would feel comfortable inside this sporty coupé, as John was more than 6ft 2in tall.

From a technical angle, the DMC-12 was not a miracle: a Renault V6 engine of 2.85-litre capacity was mounted at the rear. Initially, a mid-engine layout was designated for the car. It would allow an ideal weight distribution between axles, but, in this case, would cause the cabin to be much smaller. Therefore, John placed the engine at the very rear. This implied that the back of the car was much heavier than the front. The weight distribution ratio was 38 to 62 per cent. Most car engineers would say that was a very bad idea, but real DMC-12 fans considered the awkward weight distribution to be a big advantage.

At first, it was difficult to drive, but as you learnt to control the monster, driving – especially fast driving – became an unforgettable adventure. Taking sharp corners and flying along winding roads simulated the experience of rally driving.

The DeLorean DMC-12 undoubtedly looked like a supercar. The effect was intensified by the rear wheels being a full inch bigger than the front ones. All four wheels were equipped with disc brakes – back in 1981, this was a rarity. There was no power steering, and this peculiarity gave the driver a full connection with the road. Still, the car's opponents argued that the content of the DMC-12 didn't quite match its imposing appearance. The Renault engine was excellent, yet, for the supercar status, it was a bit too small – 130bhp was only enough to reach a top speed of 133mph. Of course, it was sufficient for sensible people, for there were not many places in the world you could safely do more than 133mph! On the other hand, the DMC-12 was quite a realistic supercar – the sort of car that didn't require much outlay for maintenance. It was an economic and practical everyday car with a unique appearance. And that was the reason why DeLorean fans were so fond of it.

But success can be a fickle friend. The deputy director of DeLorean Motor Corporation, Richard Brown, was beginning to look troubled, and he had a valid reason. At that time, Brown felt he was not a deputy director, but a nanny: a nanny for an overgrown, naughty child who spitefully refused to face the truth. Recently, John had ordered production to be increased by almost 100 per cent. Brown knew that this unreasonable request would be business suicide. The business plan was to produce no more than 8000 cars a year, as this was the optimum amount of cars that could be easily sold. If they went over this mark, they might soon find themselves on the brink of bankruptcy.

The early eighties were especially hard for the automotive industry. Even the big car producers had difficulty making ends meet. The Big Three lost four billion dollars in just two years. Meanwhile, John had succeeded in finding a magic formula, and he finished his first year as an independent car manufacturer with a remarkable profit. Now he was considering putting all his achievements at risk. Richard Brown hated to have to stand by and watch it happen, but there was nothing he could do. Quite soon after this rushed decision to increase production, John's big dream began to sink like a ship that had collided with an iceberg.

John regarded himself as a high-flier, and he couldn't switch his life down to lower revs. Accustomed to spending money when he was at General Motors, he continued to lead a similar lifestyle now that he had become self-employed. He granted himself a salary of $520,000 per year plus a bonus of $475,000. John strived for the best things in life – designer clothes, expensive shoes and jewellery. He wasn't content with the usual flight in business class any more. His friend laughed once, saying, "John, you're travelling like an oil magnate. Lucky for you that they invented the Concorde aircraft, otherwise you would have to buy a spaceship to cross the Atlantic."

"I am a magnate, too!" answered John jokingly.

To cement his great success, he decided to produce a limited edition of 100 gilded DeLoreans. Two golden beauties were assembled, and the buyers turned up instantly, keen to part with the $50,000 without batting an eyelid. Unfortunately, he fell short of the money needed to produce the remaining 98 cars. He wanted to produce a cabriolet and a five-seater sedan on the DMC-12 design basis, but these other projects went to rack and ruin as well. The company that spent its first year making a good profit was now at a deadlock.

Many people have tried to guess why DeLorean's motor plant perished. The possibility of an independent car producer surviving in a time of economical crisis was quite small, and perhaps the most tragic thing of all was the fact that DeLorean had the chance to. What John didn't know was that the corporate world was also plotting against him. Having found out that DeLorean was short on money, they devised a 'perfect' plan to remove the threat.

Meanwhile, John was planning to branch out into other activities. The man's ideas were very impressive. He wanted to buy the Jeep 4x4 cars division, the whole Chrysler factory, Lotus, Lamborghini, Alfa Romeo and other smaller companies. He wanted to merge with Ford Motors Company, and to form a joint venture with Mitsubishi, Suzuki, or Hyundai. John made preparations for geological expeditions to explore new coalfields and oil wells, to take over the fuel transit of Mexico, to import diesel engines from Europe, to produce Stirling's alternative rotary engine, to build a 4x4 vehicle plant in Poland, to reform the Romanian car industry, to produce environmentally friendly buses, to trade fashion items, to produce sunglasses, assemble radio units, and even to buy a bank. That's how wide this man's horizon was, even though the only thing the dealers and his employees wanted him to do was to focus solely on the DMC-12, and avoid thinking about other activities for at least the next couple of years.

John's wife did her best to keep out of her husband's business. She was a model and longed to become a Hollywood star. In all honesty, all this car stuff bored her stiff, yet the moment came when she realised that her husband had got himself into trouble. She tried to persuade John to see a fortune teller for advice. The unusual fact that he agreed to do it so easily only made her more concerned – it seemed that John was really desperate. A lot of people would be surprised at how many businessmen and politicians use the services of fortune tellers and astrologers. But what about John? He used to depend upon his own powers. Something had changed.

So, one fine day, he went to see Lady Sonja. The mysterious lady had arranged her office to suit a modern business woman. It was situated in Manhattan – the respectable business centre. John hesitated for a moment before entering her office. He had prepared to see an old hag in some dark place in the Bronx yet, opening the door, he found himself enveloped in a sweet-scented incense cloud. She was waiting for him, dressed in a long dark blue robe.

"Don't misunderstand me, I usually ..."

"... don't make contact with people like me?"

"That wasn't quite what I wanted to say. My wife kept going on about it until I agreed to come. However, it is only to feed her curiosity," added John timidly.

"And your own, too."

"Well, there's only one step from spirit-rapping to Satanism."

"Dogmas, dogmas, dogmas. Those are not the powers I serve." Lady Sonja didn't look offended. She observed her new client with interest.

"I was born an atheist. Cars are my religion, and all things in my life are secondary to them. It is the only religion I need. When trouble with my business started, I did a lot of thinking and began to understand many things ..."

"Yet it hasn't influenced the way you are thinking. You still regard yourself as superior to others."

"This is quite embarrassing. You don't know me at all."

"There is nothing to be embarrassed about. Your business is selling cars and my business is to look into peoples' souls. We are both professionals. Do sit down and try to make yourself comfortable. I am sure we will understand each other. It is quite possible that the answers to your problems are within reach, and you only need make a small effort to find your way."

"I have made plenty of effort lately and I doubt that anything else could help me."

"Do you want to run away?"

"I'll see it through to the end, I've nothing to be afraid of," exclaimed John resolvedly.

"Only your own insatiable pride!"

John laughed stiffly and forcedly. Could this woman see right through him?

"There is the Queen of Hearts, and the Knave of Spades next to her – the most dangerous people are those who are closest to you. Hope and modesty, hope and modesty – you have a chance to escape if you swallow your pride. I can see a very important man ... don't get yourself a new enemy, you have enough of them already."

John went away from the fortune-teller feeling dissatisfied and that it was foolish to be engaged in such shady deals. Still, worry crept into his heart. The Knave of Spades ...

Shortly after visiting the fortune teller, a little ray of hope broke through the clouds that had gathered over John's head. The phone had remained spitefully silent for some days, as if the surrounding world had disappeared and John had moved with his office into a parallel dimension, where there was no communication, intrusive reporters, or money. Suddenly, the telephone rang. It was Hoffman's cheerful, hopeful voice.

"John, you have to come to LA. There are a few people I want you to meet. It seems to me they have plenty of money and they could become your investors. Are you still interested?"

A feverish glow appeared in John's eyes. He had not slept for two nights in a row.

"James, you know, if someone told me, 'hey, I have plenty of money,' I'd follow him to the end of the world, sit on his doorstep, and not go away before I extorted a couple of million from him."

"It's all much simpler; you don't have to go to the end of the world – just be in LA tomorrow morning. We'll meet you – you must see a couple of important people."

John needed no second bidding. He rushed home to tell the grand news to his wife and to change his suit. Cristina was not at home and she hadn't even left a note. The maid couldn't give a satisfactory answer either. "Madam went out in the morning without saying a word," she told him. Did John need to worry? Not really, but deep inside his heart he felt that his family was being slowly torn apart. This wonderful woman, who appeared so reasonable and intelligent at first, seemed to have been very distant recently. How could a man let himself be fooled like this? Eleven years under the same roof and now she was behaving like a complete stranger!

"And I only understand it now, when her support is what I need most. She is somewhere, anywhere but home. However, would her presence make any difference? Would we even notice each other? We haven't had anything to talk about for a while now," thought John to himself as he went to his wardrobe.

Nothing had changed there from the crazy and vivid General Motors era – his wardrobe had more colour and flair than any other eighties man. This time, though, John chose a rather ordinary grey suit – possibly on account of his sombre mood, or in order to avoid any unwanted attention.

The next day, John arrived in Los Angeles. The ever-smiling Hoffman met him with another man in dark glasses. In a blue Cadillac, they drove towards the city centre to the Sheraton Plaza La Reina Hotel. When the threesome entered the spacious lobby, Hoffman apologised that he had to leave John for a while, to settle an important matter. The man in dark glasses glanced suspiciously at John and followed Hoffman.

John went to the restaurant and ordered a hamburger. In contrast to his extravagant life style, he didn't like gourmet food. Juvenile habits proved to be more powerful than the temptation of black caviar and shellfish. Half an hour went by and John stared intensely into his cup of coffee as if he could to see his future in there. He recalled what the fortune teller had said to him. A butler appeared at his table.

"Excuse me, Sir, are you John DeLorean?"

"Yes … at least I was him yesterday," replied John thoughtfully.

"They are waiting for you in room 511. The lift is on the left." The butler smiled and rushed away.

*The underbody of a DMC-12 shows plenty of crunch zones, making it a relatively safe car.
(Courtesy Cliff Schmucker, Patrick Conlon)*

*The underbody is being mounted on its chassis.
(Courtesy Cliff Schmucker, Patrick Conlon)*

John stood up reluctantly. He felt unwell – perhaps it was just the flight that had tired him out. John went past the lift.

"This time, I'd rather take the stairs," murmured John to himself.

He reached the fifth floor and approached room 511 slowly. What was behind that door? The answer to all his problems? Or simply yet another crazy millionaire who wished to immortalise his name on a car badge? He would soon find out. He knocked at the door and entered the room. Hoffman was there, with sleeves rolled up, fussing about. At the back of the room sat two strangers, wearing black suits. The gloomy fellow – the driver of the Cadillac – was nowhere to be seen. The two men looked suspicious, resembling either FBI agents or pimps.

"Hey, John, come in. Excuse the delay, I have a lot of business in LA and I must settle my affairs, so that both of us can return to New York this evening." Hoffman grabbed John's elbow and dragged him into another room.

"I'll brief you on the heart of the matter. Look, John, two million, which you paid into my account, may be enough to start negotiations about the administration of your company, but it will be too little for a full recovery. You understand it well yourself. However, I have a plan and I think that you'll like it. We can invest this money in one project and, in a short time, get it back with a huge profit."

"We have no time. I cannot invest my money in a risky venture and wait for a chance of profit."

"You will have to be patient for a couple of months. It is not an investment plan – it is a safe way to get the money as quickly as possible."

"James, you should have told me this yesterday and I would have saved an airfare. I can't take part in a scheme like that!"

"Wait! Heaven forbid! We have already known each other long enough. You don't think that I would try to involve you in an illegal business? Talk to these people – everything is almost settled, and all you have to do is sign a document. Your cars will be saved in no time!"

Hoffman seized the confused John by the sleeve and almost forcibly dragged him back into the big room. Both men in black turned their heads towards John at the same time, and gave him white, porcelain smiles.

"I want to introduce you to Michael Hutch and his secretary – Mr Danson. They're the people I told you about yesterday." Hoffman pointed in the direction of the two men.

John shook hands with them and they sat down at the round table. Hoffman stepped back to the door, bowed and then rattled off.

"I beg your pardon, I must rush now. I'll be back soon, John, all will be OK." He lifted his thumb theatrically and disappeared through the door.

John was standing eye-to-eye with the two shady-looking gentlemen. The silence continued for some time, and then one of the strangers began to talk.

"Mr DeLorean, firstly with your permission, I would like to express my admiration of your courage. You are an American hero indeed, because you ventured to revolt against the Big Three. What a pity that all this has turned against you. Your car is magnificent!"

"It's no big deal, I simply did what I wanted to do – whatever they write about me in the newspapers, I am a car engineer and will remain so."

"Fantastic!" exclaimed the stranger. His secretary nodded in assent. "But now, Mr DeLorean, let's move on to the matter in hand. As far as I know, Hoffman has told you in brief about the idea."

"He tried, but honestly, I didn't quite understand him." John felt uncomfortable in the company of this stranger who was flattering him. He loosened his tie and undid the shirt's top button. It seemed that both the men in black had noticed that John was nervous. They exchanged almost sympathetic glances, but the stranger continued to speak loudly and clearly, as if it were a deaf grandpa who was sitting opposite him.

"So, let's speak openly, John! You don't mind if I call you John, do you?" Without waiting for an answer, he continued. "You have two million dollars, but we have something better. Do you know – you made a mistake by calling yourself a car engineer. No, John, you are a businessman. You are a magnificent businessman, and it is widely known. You have the connections and you have the tools to sell almost anything."

John didn't like Hutch's manner. It sounded suspicious.

"I wouldn't want to get involved in any deals right now. The only thing I want is to find somebody who can help me save my company ..."

"Then you've found him," interrupted Hutch. "You won't decline my offer, I'm sure."

"Shall I call for Jacob?" Hutch's secretary suddenly asked. This small brawny man seemed very unpleasant and John noticed that he hadn't taken off his sunglasses.

"What a grand idea, Danson!"

The secretary stood up stiffly, and disappeared through the door. After a short time, he returned, accompanied by two large, muscular men. John recognised one of them – it was the Cadillac's driver. The second man looked like a nightclub bouncer. The big man took his position by the window and the room seemed to darken at once. The imposing giant crossed his fingers together, and began to flex them with unpleasant clicks. In different circumstances, John would undoubtedly have enquired where the gentleman ordered his 8XL suits, but, at this moment, his mind wasn't inclined towards sarcastic remarks. The situation grew more and more ominous. He had previously seen many different investors but this foursome by no means looked like honest businessmen. The Cadillac's driver threw a big aluminium Diplomat case onto the round table, and with a casual move, pushed a fine key into the lock. The mechanism surrendered and clicked softly. John was waiting to see what was going to happen, but the driver didn't open the case. He stepped back behind John's back, and an ominous silence set in. All John could hear was the heavy wheezing of the stranger's breath.

"He should have taken the lift, if his health is so poor," thought John to himself. He began to lose patience; it seemed that these men were playing with him. It was very strange that an experienced man like Hoffman had dragged him into this performance.

The famous silhouette of the DMC-12. (Courtesy Patrick Conlon)

Turning his scornful stare away from the security man, John noticed that Mr Hutch was gazing at him, and appealing to him benevolently to open the suitcase.

"Please, John, I want you to open it yourself. This suitcase contains the salvation of your company. Get on with it!"

John slowly moved the chair closer to the mysterious Diplomat, and reluctantly put his clammy hands on the cool metal.

"Why all this show?" he wondered. John had never liked people who beat about the bush. It was the first time he had taken part in such a strange and unconstructive business meeting. It was clear as daylight that there was no money in the case – no serious businessman would walk around with millions in a Diplomat. That sort of thing only happened in low-budget gangster movies. Maybe there was a symbolic banknote in the case? John recalled that one of his first business partners – Bart Jenkins – had given him a present of a wooden box with an old one-dollar note inside, as a symbol of their collaboration. If that was what was in the box, it was rather foolish, because these people weren't his friends.

John gripped the lid and opened it to stop this ridiculous performance. At first, he flinched and recoiled – so unexpected were the contents of the case. He wasn't prepared for such a turn. Noticing John's dumbfounded expression, the security man took a step towards the table. He opened his coat slightly, and John caught a glimpse of metal glittering on his belt. John felt frightened, possibly for the first time in his life. This feeling of fear was so rare for him – from childhood he had accustomed himself to dealing with obstacles and overcoming them bravely, at times, even recklessly. But at this moment, he needed to concentrate on how to get out of this damned hotel, rather than worrying about his failing business. Four against one – that was unfair. It was a long way to the door, and running away would be impossible. He pulled himself together, and decided to play along with his new enemies. He took one of the white bags from the Diplomat, weighed it in his hand, and laughed.

"Very well! Still, I have to be sure that this is fair play."

Mr Hutch looked contented that John had conquered his anxiety so quickly. "You shouldn't doubt our honesty. That stuff is worth $2 million. Your friend Hoffman will turn up soon with the necessary money. We'll strike a deal and you'll become the owner of this suitcase. What next? I'm sure that you'll know what to do. My dear John, you can triple your money in a short time. Isn't that what you want?"

"Of course, dear friend, I have no doubts about our deal, it's just that I have to make sure the stuff is top quality," said John, in a rather unconvincing manner. He took a pocket-knife from the table, cut the bag, and did it so clumsily that the powder spilt on his trousers. Straining his memory and trying to remember how the big guys did it in the gangster movies, John pushed his finger into the white bag and then put it to his lips. The powder left a nasty, bitter taste in his mouth. Trying to hide his awkwardness, he laughed, jumped up and exclaimed:

"It's better than gold! Much better than gold!"

That very moment, the door flew open and Hoffman appeared, accompanied by two policemen. John remained standing in the middle of the room with an open bag of cocaine in his hand. Then he put the packet on the table, and stepped back. He certainly hadn't expected the police to arrive. Hoffman's face had changed – the usual friendly smile was swapped for an icy, distant expression. Somebody got a badge wallet out of his pocket, showed it to John, and announced:

"FBI. John DeLorean, you are arrested on suspicion of drug dealing. Meyers, Mirandize the gentleman."

One of the policemen came up to John, handcuffed him and with a practiced voice, began to speak as if reading from a book:

"You have the right to remain silent. Anything you say or do can and will be used against you in court ..."

The rest just faded away from John. He was a ruined man, stitched up by his friend – this was the end. His business, his family, his reputation. How would he look Cristina and the children in the eye?

"Release on bail has been declined. The judge said that even the rich and powerful have to be responsible for their actions. I have bad news for you, John. Things are looking nasty. They have a videotape showing you declaring cocaine as better than gold, checking the quality of the stuff, lifting packages and rejoicing. What in the world were you thinking? I've known you for a long time – you're not a drug king. Were you out of your mind?" the attorney reproached John, gesticulating nervously.

John sat on the other side of the glass wall and kept silent with his head down. He couldn't quite grasp what had happened to him. Until quite recently, he had been a free man, but now he was imprisoned. Here, on this side of the glass, his life would continue for many years to come. On the other side were his business, cars, dreams, his family and friends ... It was so painful to think of this. He looked at his attorney with an absent gaze.

"No, I am not a drug king. I am a man who did his very best to save a business. But it doesn't matter now!"

"Did you really think that was the best way to save your business?"

"I told you! Why must I repeat it?" cried John. "I couldn't have behaved any differently. There were four armed men, I saw one of them brandishing a gun. I had no weapon. Are you saying I should have pretended to be a hero, and died a hero, with a bullet in my head? I did what I thought was best and I hoped I'd be able to run away at a suitable moment, but then the rat Hoffman turned up. I don't understand why he did this. We were friends."

"John, do you really think the corporate world would leave you alone, after all that has happened? After your bold public statements and that damned book you wrote? Oh, John, if only you had held your tongue. How could you have been so arrogant?"

"Nonsense! It all happened because of the car." The scales fell from John's eyes at last. "All because of the car. I was too good for them and they were frightened of me."

"Maybe, but now it's you who has to be frightened. There is a possibility you won't be a free man for a while. FBI has the evidence and facts to keep you locked up for years."

"Stop it! Oh, shut up please! They won't be able to prove my guilt. I haven't bought anything, nor have I sold anything. I haven't signed any papers, and I've never seen cocaine before this in my life. They cannot imprison me for shouting 'good as gold,' can they? I was stitched up. How could I know they were from the FBI? I thought they were regular conmen."

"Time will tell, John." The attorney shook his head. "This will cheer you up a bit though – there's somebody who wants to see you. I'll go now, I must prepare for the

INTER-OFFICE MEMO

subject file
NADA 1981

Date   February 25, 1980

To   C. R. Brown

From   John Z. De Lorean

Subject 1981 NADA Convention

Since 1981 is such a key year for us and is L.A.'s
bicentennial year, we should immediately make
rather elaborate plans for the February 7-10, 1981
NADA Convention in L.A.

Let's get a display room, reception room, and
employee rooms at the proper hotel. We will
show not only our production car but the $50,000
Golden 200 Year L.A. car, the Bugatti, and a model
of our sedan.

Please confirm our reservations as soon as
possible so we can plan effectively. I would
expect that Johnny Carson would play a very
prominent role in these activities. In effect,
this will become our major public announcement
since we can't, in advertising dollars, compete
with the industry in the fall of 1980 new car
announcement period and the holiday lull kills
coming back before February.

John Z. De Lorean

Attachment

cc: E. A. Cafiero
     C. K. Bennington
     W. F. Haddad

DE LOREAN MOTOR COMPANY

Hidden treasures of the archive – John's signature under a memo urging his senior staff to make preparations for the National Automobile Dealers Association convention the following year. It is evidence that a sedan version of DMC-12 was already on the drawing board! (Courtesy Cliff Schmucker, Patrick Conlon)

defence. From now on, you will only do what I tell you. Swallow your pride! If you want to get out of here, you will do what I say."

"Thank you, Stephen!"

Cristina appeared in the dimly lit room. She was dressed in her usual unpretentious and simple style. She held a thick grey book in her hand.

"Can you imagine?" she whispered with a sad smile. "I was searched. They thought I was hiding a revolver in the book."

"You could hide a whole policeman with full gear in a book this thick. What is it? Pulp fiction?"

"No, my love. It is a Bible. I thought you might need it now."

John looked at Cristina's pale face, perplexed. What did the woman have up her sleeve this time?

"Cris, this is very strange. Since when are you interested in things like this?"

"Since our life changed so dramatically. It will never be the same again."

"What are you trying to tell me?"

Cristina didn't answer. She cast her eyes down, for she certainly knew more than she was letting on. John glanced at the thick grey book.

"Why not? I'll read a little. Anyway, there's nothing better to do. Maybe it will take my mind off the nightmare I'm in."

Cristina looked away. Her behaviour was very strange today.

"What's wrong, Cris? You don't believe all of what's written in the newspapers, do you?"

"Yesterday they showed you on TV. Together with those gangsters ... how you're buying drugs off them. If you'd seen the crowd of journalists waiting outside our house! I could barely get out."

"So they've sniffed it out, the vultures. And you walk through a crowd of enraged journalists, holding a Bible in your hand? That must have been quite a sight. Now they'll show you on TV too," laughed John.

"I don't care."

"You'd better leave town for a while. Go away for a few weeks until everything calms down."

"No!" Cristina looked at John bravely. "I wouldn't leave you. We're family. I'll visit you as often as possible."

"You didn't answer my question."

"What question?"

"Do you think I'm involved in this drug deal?"

Cristina's eyes filled with tears. She took out a lace handkerchief from her bag and dried her eyes.

"You are involved in this deal more than you think. I spoke with your lawyer. Of course, I know you aren't guilty. I am sure you wouldn't have acted so foolishly."

"It was very important for me to hear that, Cris."

A door slammed, the warden came in and told them that the meeting was over.

"Stay strong, Johnny. I will say my prayers for you," whispered Cristina. They kissed each other through the glass and Cristina left the room, without looking back. The door closed. Freedom was somewhere far away on the other side.

Journalists were already waiting as Cristina left the building. Noticing the young woman, they immediately surrounded her. Trying to shout one another down, the journalists fired unpleasant and hurtful questions at her.

"Is it true that Mr DeLorean has admitted his involvement in a drug deal?"

"How do you feel about your husband being behind bars?"

The shouts merged into one big noisy uproar. Cristina put on her sunglasses and, accompanied by the lawyer, squeezed through the relentless crowd. Paparazzi pushed against each other in the hope of getting as close to Mrs DeLorean as possible.

The lawyer walked Cristina to his car with an anxious expression on his face, and they disappeared from the sight of the noisy mob. A few moments later, Cristina asked him to pull over.

"I'd rather go on foot, get some fresh air. I need to come to my senses."

"I promised John I'd keep an eye on you. I would strongly advise against you walking all alone in broad daylight. Remember, you are a famous person now. Your Bible-walk will be in all the newspapers tomorrow."

"Then I can still be free until tomorrow. Don't worry, everything will be OK. I have

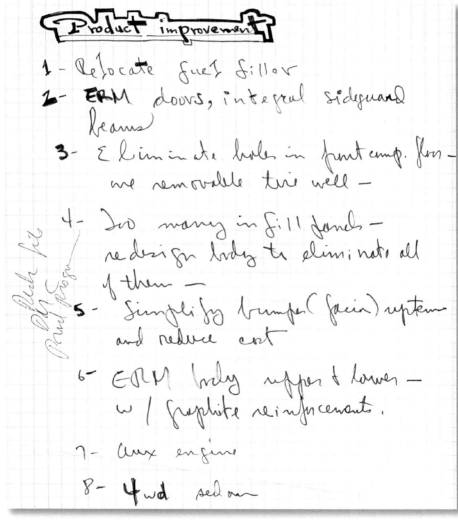

A rare document – DeLorean's handwritten to-do list. ERM here stands for Elastic Reservoir Moulding – a method of building reinforced structures from resin and foam. ERM was later found to be too expensive to use on a production car. (Courtesy Cliff Schmucker, Patrick Conlon)

to meet a friend." Cristina got out of the car, waved and disappeared. The lawyer shook his head and drove off.

Making sure that the lawyer had gone and nobody was following her, Cristina crossed the street. Covering a couple of blocks, she approached a black Buick and tapped on its roof. The lock clicked open and Cristina got into the car.

People behind bars read newspapers, too. John got the news every day and, at first, he almost enjoyed seeing himself on the front pages. "Damn it! They didn't write about me when I began building the car. Now I've been stitched up by a couple of fake gangsters in a lousy hotel and everybody's joining forces to destroy me! So that's how it is with fame? I think I'm beginning to understand it, at last," John muttered ironically.

But his feigned cheerfulness came to an end the very next day, when he noticed a photo of his wife in the newspaper. Actually there were two photos. One showing Cristina in sombre mood with a Bible in her hand, and another depicting her and a friend on a shopping trip around boutiques. "So, was she a loyal wife, or just a carefree reveller?" asked the journalists.

"What's happened?" John asked his lawyer when he came to visit.

"I've got some good news for you, John. They've released you on bail. But it isn't over yet. Brace yourself for a battle. They want to see you behind bars and they'll do anything they can to make that happen."

For the sake of appearances, John and Cristina maintained a 'business as usual' attitude. Their children continued to attend an expensive private school, while their parents carried on going to church. John was baptised in a big and touching ceremony behind his Bedminster manor; the same manor house that was now being ransacked by lawyers representing his creditors. They had a federal warrant that allowed them to search the house. They didn't leave a brick unturned. Although John had had plenty of time to 'sort' his papers before the federal warrant was issued, they still claimed they'd found certain financial documents, which suggested that something shady had gone on behind the doors of the DeLorean Motor Company.

145 creditors were snapping at his heels, the majority of them DeLorean dealers who were disappointed with the way John had handled the matter. Then there were the investors and the British government, who wanted their £130 million back. You wouldn't usually condemn a businessman for going bust – it happens every day. What made John's situation uncomfortable was the alleged double bookkeeping and money laundering. Apparently, he and Colin Chapman, along with Lotus Motors bookkeeper Fred Bushel, had been trying to conceal 18 million dollars by running the money through several offshore banks. By the time things started to come out, Chapman was already dead. Being a cautious man, John hadn't signed any documents. This meant that all responsibility fell upon Bushel. He received a three-year prison sentence. The judge passing the verdict said:

"John DeLorean should have been serving his time in Bushel's place, and I would have given him ten years."

Although potential charges of money laundering were quite serious, the cocaine deal still loomed like an axe over John's head. If found guilty, he faced 72 years in prison. And everybody, both his enemies and his friends, was convinced there was no way out of this mess. How mistaken they were. John refused to call on any witnesses, and he simplified the defence to an almost ridiculous level. John maintained that the Justice Department had set him up illegally, and, if there had been no trap, there would have been no crime. Oddly enough, this tactic worked wonders and, incredibly, John DeLorean left the court a free man. Much of the media, including *Time Magazine*, jumped eagerly on the story, and the *United Press International* still holds a piece on DeLorean's miraculous escape in its public archive.

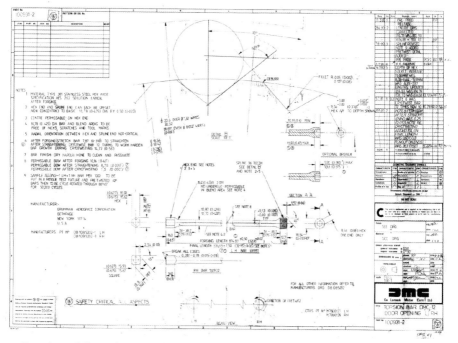

Drawing of the unique torsion bar devised by DeLorean to help open the heavy gull-wing doors. (Courtesy James Espey, DMC Texas, delorean.com)

Amidst the whirlwind of litigations, John had no time to think about his love life. Despite the new-found religion, their marriage had all but faded away, and vows they'd once made had finally lost their meaning. John and Cristina divorced in 1985, and she was free to marry Anthony Thomopoulos, the chairman of United Artists Pictures. Later, according to the media, Cristina, now John's ex-wife, claimed that she had caught John forging documents and making papers look older by holding them over a high power, electric bulb. John considered her statements hugely disloyal. He had never spoken publicly about his wife, and he obviously expected the same sort of respect from her.

The British government wanted to bring John, now tagged as a serious criminal, to justice. Neither parties had ever seen eye-to-eye, especially after the government refused to provide John with an extra loan. Although DeLorean's extradition to the UK never happened, John would never dare put a foot on British soil. There, he would remain persona non grata forever.

DeLorean's court appearances took place up until 1999. People sued him and he sued people. It was not until the turn of the century – 17 years after his dream collapsed – that DeLorean Motor Corporation was officially recognised as bankrupt. Although he still officially owed close to $100 million, John was cleared of all charges, one by one. He was a sharp man, flamboyant and maybe a bit haughty, but never a criminal. Allegedly, John's rivals 'took care' of his company once they had spotted a dangerous competitor in him; however, this is something which would be impossible to prove. We can only admire the man who tried to fulfil his dream, against all odds. The lengthy court cases hadn't drained or broken the courageous John. He considered the entire ordeal as something that had changed his life for the better.

"I think my ultimate sin was my insatiable pride. Looking back, I see that I had an arrogance that was beyond that of any other human being alive. I was a selfish person, and what has happened to me during the years has taught me that there are more important things in life than satisfying one's ambitions. Now I'm looking at my life quite differently."

Fortunately, he didn't have to overcome the difficulties on his own. Unexpectedly, as these things usually happen, Sally came into his life. An intelligent and sensible woman, she did everything she could to support her husband.

"It is foolish to mention age," John once said. He became a father once again, and remained with his wife and daughter Sheila on his New Jersey estate until he was forced out of it by the relentless creditors. Today, the posh Bedminster estate is the site of the Trump National Golf Club.

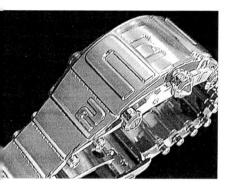

John DeLorean was fond of beautiful things. This wristwatch was his last project. (Courtesy deloreantime.com)

It has been rumoured that DeLorean was thinking about having another go at car manufacturing. Knowing him, it didn't sound at all unfeasible. He once told a friend that it would be great to build a thoroughbred sports car similar to Ferrari or Lamborghini, but more affordable. His final business venture was DeLorean Time – a company that would sell high-spec wristwatches. The prototype of the DeLorean Time wristwatch was made, but the beautiful timepiece never made it to the stores.

On March 19 2005, John died after a stroke. A couple of days later, General Motors issued a short note hailing one of the greatest executives of our times. "John DeLorean was one of Detroit's larger-than-life figures who secured a noteworthy place in our industry's history. He made a name for himself through his talent, creativity, innovation, and daring. At GM, he will always be remembered as the father of the Pontiac GTO, which started the muscle car craze of the '60s. Our thoughts today are with his family as we join them in mourning his passing."

John died amongst his family and those who loved him, so one could not really label him as a failure after all.

John DeLorean was laid to rest in Detroit; he had come full circle, back to his birthplace. He returned to the city where he had begun his extraordinary journey. The unlikely hero: a boy from a poor, uneducated family, who was so talented that he rose to the very top of General Motors management, only to quit his comfortable seat, and plunge into the unknown, to follow his dream. He was a talented engineer, a playboy, and a generator of innovative ideas. A millionaire leading a billionaire's lifestyle, an Icarus who flew too close to the sun. Unlike the legend, though, he knew how to pick himself up and carry on through life with his head held high. The dream of designing his own car never left him, and he was one of the lucky few able to fulfil this daring dream.

The Hollywood blockbuster *Back to the Future* was released in 1985, three years after John's company collapsed. The cult movie featured a DMC-12 car as one of the headlining stars. It helped to up the DMC-12's popularity to another level, and it has been on the rise ever since. After the premiere, Robert Gale, a co-screenwriter, received a letter from John DeLorean reading: "Thank you for keeping my dream alive." That illustrates just how much the car meant to John. And his dream really has been kept alive. Would you be surprised to hear that DeLorean Motor Company is up and running again? It is true. Soon after the original DeLorean Motor Company went down, Stephen Wynne spotted an opportunity to help the 9200 DeLorean owners who were left without

A replica of the DeLorean featured in the movie Back to the Future. (Courtesy Lifran, released under Creative Commons licence)

Life goes on in Texas. DMC-12s are being restored and new cars are being built here. (Courtesy DMC Texas)

service facilities. He opened a mail order parts and service facility. It grew from there, and in 1997 Stephen Wynne acquired original DeLorean stock, parts, tooling, and documentation that had originally been bought by another company. A huge facility was built in Houston, Texas and, presently, DeLorean Motor Company is the most serious DMC-12 service and restoration company in the world. It still has so-called 'new-old' stock (produced in the eighties but never used) of parts, original equipment manufactured for DMC by third party companies, and reproduction parts.

James Espey, vice president of DeLorean Motor Company, told me that the company is regularly making new DMC-12s from scratch – so the number of DeLoreans is always on the increase. It is now possible to order a brand-new DMC-12 from anywhere in the world. Since the guys from Texas have introduced right-hand-drive as an option, DeLoreans are available in the UK, Australia, and other countries. The waiting list is at least six months, and, at a base price of $57,500, it is not an overly expensive dream to follow.

Preston TUCKER

It was a sunny summer's day when Max Brinsley, a police sergeant, went on his daily patrol. There was nothing to suggest this day would be different from any other. This suburb of Memphis was as quiet and peaceful as usual, and it was unlikely that Max would have the adventure of a high-speed chase or anything similar. The heat intensified, morning clouds had broken up, and the mighty Mississippi rippled gently nearby. Max pulled off the road and stopped right by the riverside. He dismounted from the bike, stretched, and looked around. What a view! The slow river streamed majestically towards the south. Max walked along the river bank, picking up an occasional pebble and hurling it into the water. Suddenly, something big and dark lying on the bank attracted his attention. The deep brown, rounded object looked like a hippopotamus that had stretched out near the water to enjoy the rays of sun. But Max knew that hippos didn't live in Mississippi.

Forgetting about his bike and patrol duties, Max approached the strange monster. Coming closer, he realized that it was a car – or at least, what remained of a car. The policeman knew this place very well. He often came here to get away from the noise and heat of the city. This car had appeared here only recently. The policeman touched the warm metal and he was seized by a strange feeling. Examining the rusty old object, he realised that he had never seen anything like it before, despite his interest in cars. The brown car was long and low-slung and its proportions were very strange. Judging from the appearance of the front, there should have been three headlamps. All the glass was missing, but the body was in comparatively good condition. Max noticed a small oblong badge on the car's back wing. He tried to clean it with his sleeve and soon it was possible to read the inscription quite clearly: Tucker. He recalled the name instantly. He had seen it in a magazine as a child. Tucker was a talented engineer whose car factory went bankrupt because of a shameful conspiracy.

The policeman understood immediately how valuable his find was. Without hesitation he ran to his bike, started it up, and sped off in the direction of the city. An hour later, he returned with a police trailer. It turned out that his job in the police had some privileges – Max's colleagues never questioned why he suddenly needed a trailer. Attaching the Tucker to the trailer, he went home. It was lucky no-one else had found the car before him. He placed the wrecked car in his back yard and rushed back towards his office. He didn't want his boss to notice that he was off patrol.

Max rode his bike along the suburban streets of Memphis, but he could think of nothing except that old car. He imagined how he would start the restoration work, how he'd try to source the spares, and how he'd take part in car shows. Then suddenly, something large pulled out from a side street ...

Max regained consciousness in the hospital ward. His leg was in plaster and hoisted somewhere up by the ceiling, his head was bandaged, and a hammer was banging between his ears. A worried doctor stood by his bed.

Preston Tucker in the early 1940s.
(Courtesy Ypsilanti Historical Society,
ypsilantihistoricalsociety.org)

"It's a miracle that you survived after such a terrible crash. You will have to stay in the hospital for at least a month."

"I'll have to postpone the restoration," thought Max, "a month isn't such a long time. The car won't disappear. If it survived 30 years, it will survive another month."

But there he was mistaken. When his colleagues brought him home after a month, the car had indeed disappeared. Questioning his neighbours didn't help – they hadn't even noticed that the wreck had been in Brinsley's back yard. The gate was locked up as usual; there was no sign of a break-in. The car had vanished as if it had been a wraith. More than twenty years have passed since that mystical event. Nobody has ever seen the car again, within the neighbourhood or anywhere else. How could it disappear from a courtyard with a high fence and locked gate? What was its fate? Who knows?

Preston Tucker – the inventor of this car – had a strange fate, too. If sheer enthusiasm was enough to tip the world off its axis, then Tucker would have made it revolve in the opposite direction. Unfortunately, as is often the case, good intentions are not enough to realise ambitious goals – somebody will always put a spanner in the works.

The world of motors became familiar with Preston Tucker during the early 1920s. The young man could always be seen hanging around where there were motors roaring and rubber burning. He certainly had a bee in his bonnet about cars. You couldn't possibly miss him – he was more than six feet tall, hat tipped back and sleeves rolled up, dressed elegantly, regardless of whether or not he had money. He was a fervent Indy racing fan, and it was quite obvious that he was longing to swap a spectator's seat for an insider's place. Preston loved to drive cars, but he loved improving and building them even more. He always found room for improvement, even for a mechanism that was close to perfection. His apartment looked more like the warehouse of an engineering office; crammed with rolls of technical drawings and piles of Da Vinci-style sketches, understandable only to himself.

Preston's first job was as an errand boy in the huge Cadillac enterprise. His task was to run along the endless corridors between different departments, delivering documents, notes, drafts, etc. It was very tiresome and rather boring, but Preston wouldn't have been Preston if he hadn't come up with a plan to ease his day. Roller skates made things quicker and meant he didn't get so tired. He rolled through the Cadillac factory, scaring his colleagues and giving the occasional pinch to any good-looking secretaries. He mastered skating so well that he would have been the envy of modern skater boys. However, one day, his easy time at Cadillac came to an abrupt end when, after one particularly sharp corner, he ran into a big, plump figure. When both collision victims got up, it turned out that the big, plump figure was none other than his boss ... Tucker had to leave his beloved job and exchange his roller skates for a policeman's whistle.

His police service coincided with the turbulent prohibition period in the USA. There were the daring Canadian bootleggers, and the elegant gentlemen who wore spats and gathered in speakeasies late in the evening to sip whiskey and rum from white coffee cups. There were gangsters, street shootings, high-speed pursuits – it was an exciting yet dangerous time. Preston Tucker was the scourge of the bootleggers in and around Detroit. He took his duties very seriously. The liquor smugglers who arrived from Canada in large numbers didn't get any mercy from the young policeman – he was an incorruptible man, and he put dozens of bootleggers behind bars. In fact, he wasn't liked by the mob or his fellow policemen. People like him were undesirable in the police force – he was too alert, and prevented his colleagues from striking shady deals with smugglers. The boss was on a constant lookout to find a reason to get rid of the enthusiastic Preston. Soon, he had his chance.

Tucker was very keen on weapons; he had a revolver that he could dismantle and reassemble in a few seconds, and he could use a gun better than a hero in a Western. Tucker was confident of his knowledge of cars, and he decided to make some improvements to an old patrol car. A good hole in the collector would, in his mind, eliminate the defect in the cooling system. As he didn't have his set of tools to hand, he decided to shoot the hole with his revolver. Unauthorised shooting in the police station was enough to see him go. Still, he remained fond of weapons and cars all his life.

Tucker took a job in the Studebaker car factory. Part of his duty was to actually sell cars, and he took to this job like a duck to water. Being persistent, determined, and, in certain cases, rather stubborn, he was able to sell almost anything to anyone. It was said about him that he would walk any distance to reach his goal.

In 1935, Tucker became a significant figure behind the scenes of Indy 500 racing. Together with his partner, Harry Miller, he was a joint owner of the racing team Tucker-Miller. They succeeded in making ten excellent racing cars. The Ford company supplied the engines for these, but Tucker was never satisfied with what Ford provided, and kept adjusting and improving them. Through a mutual acquaintance, Tucker and Miller were then brought in to assist in the rescue of a then-famous car producer, Marmon. The company had won the first-ever Indy 500 car race, but struggled big time after the Great Depression. Its cars were too expensive for late thirties America.

The Second World War upset Tucker's racing plans, but he managed to innovate once again. He built an ideal combat vehicle prototype, called simply the 'Combat Car,' and offered it to the US government. The 'heavies' were one of the weakest links of the Allies' equipment – American tanks hadn't come too far from the standards of the European machinery used during the First World War. Tucker's monster was super modern, and too advanced for its time. Today's tanks are still plagued by the same old problem of being too heavy and too slow. Hence, they cannot achieve what the Combat Car could back in 1940. Tucker's machine could do over 100mph, had high carrying capacity and good road quality, yet the government still refused the project. "This vehicle is too fast for us to use in combat situations." That was the official response from the US government. Today's fastest tank is the British Scorpion, and the unofficial speed record is 60mph – still a long way short of Tucker's Combat Car.

Despite all that, Preston still managed to go down in the military history books. Swallowing the rejection of the Combat Car project, he constructed a revolving turret that could be used on battle planes to make aiming and shooting easier. A gunner could sit inside the turret, stick a machine gun through a special aperture, and fire at the enemy. The magical turret was produced in Tucker's own factory, the Ypsilanti Machine and Tool Company.

The war came to an end, and Tucker, understanding that he wouldn't make it big as a military engineer, decided to focus on cars again. The car industry in the USA had almost been destroyed by the war. In accordance with the resolution of the US Congress of 1943, production of passenger cars was prohibited. Everyone had to concentrate on the military effort. Fuel was rationed, and tyres and oil were so expensive that only the rich could afford to drive a car. In 1945, when rationing ended and the government allowed factories to make cars again, the Americans realised that they had nothing to drive. By the end of the year, the Big Three (Ford, General Motors and Chrysler) had only managed to produce 700 new cars. During the years of war, the passenger fleet of the USA had shrunk by 4 million units. President Roosevelt raised the alarm.

"We need ten million new cars and quickly, otherwise America will be faced with a crisis."

The producers didn't have the time to design new models, so they just scrubbed the rust from their prewar conveyors and continued to produce old, outdated cars. Tucker looked down his nose at all this fuss. "I want to produce a car that will go from zero to 60mph in ten seconds and with a top speed of 100mph. You will have never seen anything this progressive and impressive," he announced to the press. The Big Three just laughed at his extravagance. "This is not the first Indy 500 engineer to have gone mad after the war."

Chaos ruled in postwar America, and there was a cartload of swindlers who promised to build up the new America and raise spirits to an unprecedented height. For that very reason, people regarded any audacious assertions and promises with a certain degree of scepticism. But Preston's fervent enthusiasm had begun to gather momentum.

Nobody was happy about the Big Three offering prewar models for sale. Now there was an attractive, articulate person, promising to make the whole driving process a fairytale experience by making a supercar affordable to any middle-class American family. Wasn't that just wonderful? Tucker had assured that his car would cost no more than $2450. That was at a time when new cars seldom came for less than $4000.

With his public speeches and tireless energy, Preston Tucker managed to capture the interest of a lot of people. In 1946, he founded a joint-stock company. He miraculously sold shares in a company that existed only on paper, and whose real value was zero. To get extra funds, he sought for potential dealers and offered them the rights to sell a car that didn't yet exist. He didn't even have drawings to show his investors. Still, mainly thanks to Tucker's spotless reputation, and his gift of the gab, he found plenty of people who would agree to invest their hard-earned money into Tucker's dream – an invisible figment of his imagination, like a soap-bubble that could burst at any moment. It should be mentioned that not for a moment did Tucker think about swindling people and abusing their trust. No, Tucker wasn't a cheat. He believed in his dream, and he was fully confident that in no time at all, he would construct the very best car the world had ever seen. He was sure that in ten years' time, he would launch his company alongside the Big Three and one of the current automotive giants would bite the dust.

Having sold his dream to risky investors and dealers for a couple of million, Tucker realised that all doors were open to him and his hands were, for once, untied. But hold on a moment! A small detail was missing – he still had no car. And there was another thing he had not considered – it had never even crossed his mind that the Big Three and the American government might have a different vision of the development of the car industry, and that a man like Tucker, who had no connection with underground organisations and money laundering schemes, was very undesirable to corporate

The beginning. This is how Preston Tucker imagined the car's design in 1946. It was hugely improved upon within the next year.
(Courtesy Science Illustrated (defunct))

America. I should point out that the president of the USA, Franklin Roosevelt, would have liked to have seen the Big Three disseminate – he hated big corporations. Hence, companies like Tucker's were considered very important for the development of the new US economy. However, it almost seemed as if the course of the postwar economy was not conducted from the White House, but from Detroit – the capital of the car industry.

In the postwar years, the government began selling off the military works that now stood empty. Preston Tucker was lucky enough to get hold of one of those works. The production footage was almost a whopping 40 hectares, making his new property near Chicago one of the biggest industrial buildings in the world. During the war Dodge had been making aircraft engines there, but, as the Allies marched back home victorious, Dodge abandoned the premises because they were too expensive to maintain. Besides, this industrial estate was built using the US military budget.

Having landed such a bargain, Tucker infuriated his mighty rivals. Ford had anticipated acquiring the same factory but the presidential policy was strict – only small and medium-sized businesses were entitled to cheap industrial property. Another similarly imposing plant was bought by Kaiser. This one, however, didn't live up to expectations, and in 1955 Kaiser, the maker of attractive yet inexpensive cars, ceased production there. Many years later, Ford eventually got its hands on the (by then) former Tucker Motors plant, split it in two, and built a posh Ford City Shopping Centre mall.

Back in 1946, though, Tucker had raised enough money and acquired an excellent motor plant, but he still didn't have a car to build. He had to step up to the plate to keep his good reputation. He hastily hired Alex Tremulis as chief designer of Tucker Corporation. He had made some excellent designs for Auburn and Duesenberg before

An early illustration that Preston Tucker fed to several magazines and newspapers. (Courtesy Alden Jewell)

the war, and was involved in military machinery design during hostilities. Alex was given just six days to perfect Tucker's drawings and come up with the final design of what was destined to be the car of tomorrow.

Tremulis was a bit of a jester, and an enthusiastic ufologist, too. In his spare time he drew various flying objects. His colleagues said that Tremulis had an inexhaustible imagination. He could always draw an original flying saucer which was completely different from the one that he had drawn the day before. Even the Martians would have been envious of his designs. It is rumoured that a certain amount of UFO photographs that were 'leaked' into the press, were actually the creative work of the cheeky Alex Tremulis. He often authored photo-collages that depicted UFOs over popular places in America. It is just possible that Tremulis is one of those responsible for the UFO-mania of the 1950s, and the hobby ufologists who still keep old newspaper cuttings with information about odd flying objects are simply naïve victims of the fun-loving Tremulis. Eventually, the merry designer was able to express his imagination in a rather more significant type of work. He took part in the Space Shuttle type rocket design program.

The designer was of the opinion that the future of space exploration would belong to a spaceship that takes off from a launch pad, but lands just like an ordinary airplane, gliding horizontally. It turned out that he was right, and the famous reusable spacecraft has retained some features that were designed by Alex Tremulis.

So, the two nonconformist thinkers had found one another. Alex Tremulis immediately latched on to Tucker's crazy ideas and far-fetched plans. They thought alike, and soon after meeting each other they a shared vision of what the car of tomorrow should look like. In just six days, Tremulis completed a car design that would excite people for many years to come. When Alex showed his final design to Preston Tucker, the boss was thrilled – his dream car was reflected back at him from the sheet of paper. The men set to work immediately.

As a general rule of thumb, a brand new car is usually modelled in clay first, then the press-forms are made from the full-size clay model. In 1946, it was almost impossible to get hold of modeller's clay in the USA, and they hardly had enough time to mess around with it anyway. The men made the car from scratch using just bare tin sheets, wood hammers and basic metalworking tools. Possibly, it was the first and definitely one of the last attempts in car history to make a prototype of a production car without using a life size model, so good were his metalworkers.

Meanwhile, Americans, especially the investors and dealers, started to kick up a fuss about the promised car. The result of all the publicity was that people all across the country knew about Tucker's plans to make a brand new car. Tucker realised that he wouldn't be able to construct his own engine, so he had to think of another way to power his car. It wouldn't be right to use a well-known engine of Detroit make. Firstly, by doing that, he would admit that his competitors were capable of making a good engine; secondly, Tucker was sure that the mainstream car engines were no good for his supercar. There were some good ones produced across the pond in Europe, but they were too expensive and not efficient enough. So, what to do now? The answer to his plea came from the sky – a beautiful and fast Bell's helicopter flew over Chicago. This was just what Tucker needed – an engine that had undergone rigorous tests and had even endured the war. Tucker approached Bell and ordered six-cylinder opposite engines. I bet they looked at him strangely – yes, many motor sports enthusiasts bought opposite engines for their hot rod monsters, but a helicopter engine in the back of a mass-produced car? That was a mad thing to do! However, the press and public picked up on the idea and simply loved it. They really didn't see anything wrong with that. Now the whole country was talking about the wonderful car with a helicopter engine.

Even though Bell's engine was as close to perfection as the year 1946 permitted, Tucker didn't find it good enough. It used air cooling, and overheated relatively quickly and started losing power. Placing this 'thermal powerhouse' in the back of a passenger car would mean turning its interior into a greenhouse. It wouldn't be possible to stay inside, because, after some ten miles or so of cruising, the passengers would need to jump out and cool off. Being a clever engineer, Tucker quickly found a solution to this problem. He rebuilt the engine so that it would function with a water heating system.

Tucker was sorry that his old friend Harry Miller couldn't take part in his great adventure – Miller died in 1943. But another friend from the carefree Indy 500 times was safe and sound – John Eddie Offutt. He was the guru who, back in the thirties, built a car that won Indy 500 twice, and he now worked with Tucker's new car.

When the car was finally complete, Tucker knew that all his bragging over the last two years had been justified. The six-cylinder helicopter engine was very powerful. With a capacity of 5.5 litres, it produced power of 166bhp and 504Nm torque. That level of torque is a rarity even in contemporary cars, but for 1947, these technical specifications

The grand opening of the Chicago plant, with Tucker's mechanics at the centre of attention. (Courtesy Ypsilanti Historical Society, Gerry Pety & Derek Spinei)

were sensational. As Tucker promised, the car could reach 60mph in just 10 seconds. In those days, even half a minute was not bad at all for an average car.

Tucker named his masterpiece the Tucker 48, after the year it came into production. Most people referred to it as the Tucker Torpedo, though. That was the name of the hand-drawn prototype that appeared in the *Science Illustrated* magazine in December 1946. Later, Preston Tucker often called the car the Torpedo – after all, it sounded more impressive. Moreover, the car justified its new name – it could reach a top speed of 124mph.

Tucker's attention to detail was truly amazing. The front and rear seats were identical. Tucker thought that it was necessary to swap the front and rear seats once every 6 months to even out the wear. The front seats usually wore sooner than the rear seats, because they had to bear the weight of passengers more often than the rear. Considering that it was still 1948, Tucker's car was too good for its time. Nobody could really appreciate the features Tucker was offering. Really, what could the average American, who had just endured the war, make of a car with an independent suspension for all four wheels and a 100 per cent hermetic water cooling system? What benefit would he get from the third headlamp that turned with the steering wheel, shedding light into the forthcoming turn? Those technical innovations looked good on the pages of *Science Illustrated,* but they hardly impressed the buyers – actually, the first thing they usually noticed was the interesting appearance of the car. Compared with other cars of that era, the Tucker Torpedo looked tremendous. It was long (18ft 3in) and quite low (5ft). The car's proportions were strikingly different from its competitors. The cab was stretched forward and the car looked dynamic, even when it was standing still.

Tucker had designed his car with a low body, to keep the drag coefficient as low as possible – the C_d stood at 0.30. It is an excellent coefficient, even by today's standard, and many contemporary cars struggle to achieve that figure. As a result of the low drag coefficient, and some clever tinkering, the car did 21-26mpg, whereas its rivals averaged around 9-15mpg. Some of the credit must go to the Bell's engine, too. Who said that a helicopter engine was meant to be heavy and gas-guzzling? Just the opposite in fact – aircraft engineers have always done their best to keep the weight down and increase the flying range. Bell's helicopter engine was made of aluminium and weighed only 320lb. A Buick V6 of the same period, for example, weighed 414lb!

The car made its official debut in the summer of 1947. The first example that was shown to investors, dealers and journalists was lovingly named the Tin Goose by Preston Tucker. Funnily enough, the first car was not complete when it was publicly shown. It was possible to start the car, and you could drive it to your heart's content,

A happy family – Preston Tucker with his wife Vera and children at the Torpedo launching party. (Courtesy Ypsilanti Historical Society, Gerry Pety & Derek Spinei)

A fragment from Tucker sales brochure. (Public domain image)

The Tucker '48 ... The Car You Have Been Waiting For

but, alas, it couldn't go in reverse. The gearbox lacked the reverse gear. Even though it seemed only Tucker himself and a couple of his companions knew about this little hitch, the rumour spread like wildfire, and, the very next day, the whole country knew that the famous Tucker Torpedo could not go backwards. Of course, very soon the gearbox problem was fixed, and all Torpedos switched swiftly from forward to backward motion, but the legend about the car that couldn't go backwards still lives on. The chairman of the Tucker Car Club is still approached by strangers who ask:

"Oh, so this is the car that doesn't go in reverse?"

"Well, actually, it does now."

"Oh really?!"

After a short period of trepidation, the nation forgot about the Tucker's technical imperfections. Not everyone paid attention to the rumours, anyway. Acclaim came later that year when the Torpedo was exhibited at a gallery in New York. The general public had a chance to see the beautiful car, and then Tucker-mania kicked off. Anyone who took the slightest interest in automobiles talked about nothing else but the unique and brilliant Tucker Torpedo. The big car producers couldn't get used to this new situation, and began to use unfair methods to undermine Preston Tucker. Soon enough, Tucker discovered that his factory had been infiltrated by a spy. This person was removed from the premises, but Tucker refused to sue him. He thought that suing would be futile. He didn't want to hide anything that went on behind the doors of his innovative 'car lab.' According to him, although the Torpedo was crammed full of technical innovation, none of the Big Three companies would be bold enough to use helicopter motors, disc brakes, and independent suspension on their pathetic production cars.

Maybe that was his mistake. Tucker had taken a big risk and he knew it. He was permitted to use the big Chicago plant by the US Military Administration, which provided the premises on the condition that Tucker raise $15 million start-up capital over a short period of time. The Administration was in charge of all former military factories in the US, and it took good care to distribute the industrial buildings to competent people who would help kick-start the national economy. It had implicit faith in Tucker – a man without a penny to his name. However, by selling franchises to interested car dealerships, he raised only $6 million. He had to find at least a further $9 million to start mass production. The US Securities and Exchange Commission took an interest in the 'shady' selling of Tucker's franchises in 1946. A little later, it would play a major part in reducing Tucker to ruin: now, however, it simply conducted a thorough investigation.

Tucker's actions were not considered criminal – there's nothing wrong in selling franchises. This time, he escaped with frayed nerves and a little shadow on his reputation, although it was still clean enough to continue with his work. As his popularity grew, he began receiving offers from potential investors who were ready to give him the money immediately. Unofficially, the Big Three showed interest in acquiring rights to the Torpedo. It goes without saying that Preston, being Preston, rejected all their advances. He knew that the very moment he took the bait from the bigger companies, he would lose control over his own company. No, that was not good enough for him. Meanwhile, time raced by and there was still no money.

Preston Tucker launched an unprecedented campaign. At the end of 1946, he floated shares of a nonexistent company. Tucker's idea was to sell shares of his company to raise $20 million. He wasn't looking for big investors, so he invited the general public to become a part of his enterprise and form the future of the American car industry.

At the same time, Tucker found his first serious problem in the shape of Wilson Wyatt, head of the National Housing Agency. Wyatt allegedly had his eye on the huge Chicago plant. Why use it for a car factory? He thought it would be far better suited to making prefab houses. Wyatt pulled the right strings in Washington, and the War Assets Administration received a signal to cancel Tucker's lease and hand the premises to the Lustron Corporation. It was clear as day that Wyatt had an interest in the Lustron Corporation.

Having spotted corruption, Tucker didn't keep quiet, for he didn't fear anything. If somebody like him were alive today, he would end up with a bullet in his head, but postwar America was not that way inclined. The corporate world had other weapons in its arsenal – namely, a close relationship with the government and its thinly disguised corruption. There were very few ways to the top, and the easiest way was to make friends with the right people. So much for the American dream!

Fortunately, the War Assets Administration didn't give in to the pressure; it actually extended the start-up capital deadline. Soon, Tucker found himself another powerful and influential enemy – the Michigan state senator, Homer Ferguson, who allegedly influenced the investigation and contributed to the defamation of Preston Tucker.

A Christmas greeting from Preston Tucker. (Courtesy Alden Jewell)

Eventually, Tucker succeeded in selling the shares of his company. Despite this, by early 1948, his pockets were empty once again – the money had been spent in perfecting the prototype and equipping the motor plant. In this emergency situation, Preston had to come up with a stroke of genius to survive – and he did. Tucker began to sell accessories for his non-existent car. "If you buy my car, you will need a car radio and seat covers." America had never seen anything like that before. The press picked up on it immediately and jeered at Tucker for a good couple of months. They made fun of his shamelessness, but all they were doing, in fact, was giving him free publicity and advertising space, which was just what he needed!

People were inspired by all the publicity and started buying the radio units and seat covers. In a few months, he managed to get together about $2 million. His enemies were on alert too. People who had attempted to ruin his reputation some time ago now started asking new questions about the legality of selling people the accessories. The Securities and Exchange Commission swarmed over Tucker's factory, which by then had started up the production line. They forced him to stop production and dismiss every one of his 1600 workers.

On June 15 1948, some of the biggest national newspapers printed a copy of Preston Tucker's open letter addressed to the government and his competitors, in which he appealed from 'Philip drunk' to 'Philip sober'. It later turned out that 'Philip' chose not to be sober, unfortunately.

"Gentlemen," Tucker wrote to the Big Three. "As you know, we are building a completely new motorcar – the rear-engine Tucker. Being newcomers in the field, we have had to start from scratch and work harder and faster than most of you. For example, instead of the 20 months one usually needs to produce a new model of conventional design, my engineers have taken less than 10 to perfect a car which I firmly believe will be the beginning of a whole new era in motoring.

An early advertisement shows the Torpedo in exaggerated detail.
(Courtesy Alden Jewell)

"In this same year, we have completed a nationwide dealer organisation, acquired the largest, most modern automotive plant in the world, and cleared the decks for mass production. These things have been done – and done well – in spite of persistent and unfair opposition from within the automotive industry.

"Please don't misunderstand me. Many of you have gone out of your way to be friendly towards the Tucker Corporation. It's true that some of you do not share our

A magnificent frontal view of a Torpedo. (Courtesy Norm Hoekstra)

From a helicopter to a car: the unique opposite engine. (Courtesy Norm Hoekstra)

conviction that a rear-engine car is the car of the future, but you have been willing to let the American motorist judge that for himself, in the firm belief that what's best for the motorist is best for you, in the long run.

"But there is another group – a very powerful group – which for two years has continued with a carefully organised campaign to prevent the motoring public from ever getting behind the wheel of a Tucker.

"These people have tried to introduce spies into our plant. They have endeavoured to bribe and corrupt loyal Tucker employees. Such curiosity about what goes on in the Tucker plant should be highly flattering, I suppose. But they haven't stopped there.

"They even have their spokesmen in high places in Washington. As a direct result of their influence, Tucker dealers all over the country – men of character and standing in their communities – have been harassed and grilled by agents of the government, and Congressional Investigating Committees.

"My associates and myself and the Tucker Corporation have been investigated, time and again. Millions of dollars of the taxpayers money have been squandered in an utterly fruitless effort to kill the Tucker, to bar us from needed raw materials, to keep us so busy defending ourselves and our efforts that the motoring public would tire of waiting for a completely new rear-engine car. But they haven't been able to stop us.

"You know, perhaps, that our bid on a government-owned steel plant in Cleveland was recently refused. Let me tell you the inside story of that. Sealed bids were called for, in accordance with law. Only two were submitted, one by the steel company operating the plant, the other by the Tucker Corporation. The bids were opened nearly five months ago. The Tucker Corporation's bid was high. If Tucker's bid had been accepted, it could have given taxpayers as much as four million dollars more for the plant than the steel company offered.

Tucker Torpedo's engine bay and the magnificent chrome details.
(Courtesy Norm Hoekstra)

"This plant would have provided ample raw materials for high-volume production of the Tucker and would have served numerous small businesses, now starving for steel.

"You would think our high bid for the plant would have been accepted long ago. For five months, political pressure, ruthless and barefaced, has forced delay after delay. We're still waiting. We don't know who is responsible for this. But who do you suppose is getting the raw material from this plant we want for Tucker and other small businesses? None other than some well known – and unfriendly – automotive manufacturers.

"Most of the political pressure and investigations we have had to face these last two years can be traced back to one influential individual, who is out to 'get Tucker.' If he acts out of honest conviction in his efforts to prolong the debut of the motorcar, then I hope he will have the courage to tell the public just that.

"But personally, we believe he has more obvious motives. Evidence in Tucker files, for example, shows the controlling interest from a large sales agency of an automotive corporate subsidiary is in his wife's name. And when he gave an elaborate party at a Washington hotel a few months ago, who do you suppose paid the bill? None other than an official of an automobile manufacturer – a manufacturer who has been distinctly unpleasant towards the Tucker Corporation. Is all this, too, just a coincidence?

"Now, once more, we are being investigated. Just at a time when we are starting up production on a car that has won the hearts of the million motorists who have seen it, just when the job of making automobiles demands all our time and energy, my

A front-engine conversion of a Tucker Torpedo. (Courtesy Norm Hoekstra)

associates and I are asked to take time out again and again for these investigations, ever since we had the temerity to suggest America is eager for a completely new car.

"What would you think in our place? Would you say it was just coincidence – or would you think it was planned that way?

"You wonder, perhaps, why I have made these statements in an open letter. Here's why; as President of the Tucker Corporation, I'm responsible to 1872 Tucker dealers and distributors and nearly 50,000 Tucker stockholders. These people have invested $25,000,000 into the Tucker Corporation. And I intend to protect their interests.

"In addition, we have promised American motorists a completely new rear-engine motorcar, and hundreds of thousands have written to us and said that they are ready and waiting to buy it. Every day, letters come to us from people who know that, in fighting to put the rear-engine Tucker on the road, we are, at the same time, fighting for their right as motorists to get the finest engineering American ingenuity can produce.

"We are going to justify the support these motorists have so generously given us. We are going to give them the car they want at a price they can afford, and without paying tribute to the Black Market. How this will be done will be announced today.

"But, in the meantime, I want to register the fact that we have only just begun to fight. We have been patient so far, but our patience is wearing thin. We can give names, dates and places to prove our charges of unfair competition, and if necessary we will do it.

"If the day comes when anyone can bend our country's laws and lawmakers to serve selfish, competitive ends, that will be the day our democratic government dies. And we're just optimistic enough to believe that once the facts are on the table, American public opinion will walk in with a big stick."

Tucker Torpedo: a view from the rear. (Courtesy Norm Hoekstra)

This letter perfectly showcases Tucker's feelings. His health worsened because of severe stress. All the people who read his open letter totally sympathised with the unfortunate businessman; however, the media wasn't as influential as it is now. There was nothing to do but watch the Big Three and the government trample on the brilliant dreams of Preston Tucker. Soon public opinion began to divide and, as often happens, people turned their back on their hero.

Having scented out trouble, the dealers, who had acquired a licence to sell Tucker's cars, brought a court case against Preston Tucker. A string of tiresome court appearances followed. In the end, Tucker, helped by some good lawyers, succeeded in proving that Tucker Motor Corporation was able to function, that his car existed, and that the production line was ready to roll. The accusations against Tucker were simply ridiculous. An experienced judge did his best to try to prove that the car that they'd been talking about didn't exist at all. The reality was that the Commission stopped a fully functional production line with 51 Torpedos assembled and ready.

If the Commission had intervened a little bit earlier, the judge would have been right. The most heartbreaking thing of all is the story of the Tucker's devoted men who, in spite of dismissal and the official closure of the production line, still continued assembling the car secretly within the limits of possibility. They would have assembled even more cars if they hadn't run out of raw materials. At the time of the Commission's intrusion, only a couple of Torpedo cars were ready. The boss had fascinated his workers with his idea to a point where they couldn't leave those wonderful cars half-finished. Had they done otherwise, there would be nothing to show for Tucker's ordeal today and all his work would have ended up in a scrapyard.

Even though the court knew that the cars were real, the judge stubbornly stuck to his opinion. Then, having realised that the prosecution hung by a thread and was minutes away from being discredited, he turned his coat and claimed that the Tucker

Stylish minimalism: the dashboard of Torpedo. (Courtesy Norm Hoekstra)

Torpedo didn't tally with the initial description in the advertisement. Preston Tucker was tagged a liar, and his behaviour was classified as dishonest competition. Seven Torpedo cars were given to independent experts, so that they could test the cars on the Indianapolis race route. Their verdict was unanimous – the Tucker Torpedo was a high-quality engineering product, and the power, torque and other specs completely tallied with figures mentioned in sales brochures. The case was disproved once again. In January 1950, Tucker and his companions were completely acquitted, but it was impossible to salvage the company after such a long stoppage. The Tucker Motor Corporation property was sold by auction at ridiculous prices. Even though Tucker was acquitted, he knew that after what he had learnt about the corporate 'mob,' his engineering and entrepreneurial career could not continue in the USA. He would struggle to find a job on a milk float now, not to mention in the car industry. For that reason, the most sensible thing to do was to set up a new business in another country, turn over a new leaf and start from scratch. Preston Tucker chose sunny Brazil, the exact opposite to the world he had known before; the world that had brutally trampled on his dreams with dirty, corporate boots.

Having barely rested after the ordeal of recent years, he started on a new endeavour. Tucker wasn't the type of person who would easily resign himself to fate. He used to say "I never give up, and I never will." He still believed that, sooner or later, he would own a car factory and build affordable cars for the pleasure of others.

Tucker began work on a new project called the Carioca, an extraordinary two-seater sports car. Stylistically, it echoed the lines of the Torpedo, but the Carioca was much smaller, with a slender boat-shaped body and open wheels. Some say that the Plymouth Prowler was inspired by the Carioca. Tucker started working on the new model in 1951. He had found some investors and was busy forming the team. It turned out that the life of this car was even shorter than that of Torpedo.

No engine here: the huge trunk of the Tucker Torpedo. (Courtesy Norm Hoesktra)

In the mid-'50s, doctors diagnosed Tucker with lung cancer. The Carioca never even made it off the drawing board, although he had found an investor in South America, and the car was being prepared for production. Tucker died four days before New Year, 1957. Sadly, his dream will remain unfulfilled.

Tucker's nephew, in family circles known as Uncle Tom, told me that the Carioca was almost ready when Preston died. "Preston was very serious about the Carioca. I've seen designs that he was working on in 1956, prior to his health getting really bad. Preston's lead person in South America was a man named Max Garavito. He owned a large magazine business in South America and was very connected to the business community there. Max had a big moustache and looked like the Cisco Kid's partner Pancho, if you've ever seen the series."

Today, the price of a Tucker Torpedo would be well over $500,000, but it is almost impossible to find one in antique car auctions. One of the more recent sales took place in 2008, and saw a Torpedo go for over a million dollars.

The Smithsonian National Museum of American History got hold of a Torpedo thanks to a curious coincidence. In 1992, the unique car with serial number 1039 (the thirty ninth of fifty one cars) was confiscated from a drug king during a raid. Due to its cultural importance, the car was then given to the museum.

At least some of the current owners of the legendary car still use it, and there have been reports that it is still capable of its top speed, despite its age.

As sad as it may be, it is clear that there will never be any more Tuckers made. For people who cannot accept the bitter truth, there is always an alternative. Ida Inc, mainly known as a hot-rod customs producer, also does a Torpedo replica. For as

Preston and Vera Tucker in August 1956, with their grandchildren.
(Courtesy Ypsilanti Historical Society, Gerry Pety & Derek Spinei)

little as $100,000, you can get a Torpedo lookalike crafted in glass fibre, and equipped with a modern car engine. Surprisingly, this company receives very few orders. Nevertheless, the Tucker Torpedo is sacred to many Americans, especially those who loathe the corporate world. Tucker is like Niagara Falls, Captain America or Route 66 – one of the things that makes Americans extremely proud. Meanwhile, there is always somebody suggesting that the Tucker Motor Corporation will be resurrected to produce a modernised version of the Torpedo. However, in the last few years, this idea seems to have been nothing more than rumour. Who knows? Similar experiments of reviving an old car marque have been seen before.

Preston Tucker was a unique man. More than 50 years have passed since his death. He managed to build just 51 cars, yet still the Tucker Car Club has more than 600 active members. They are historians, engineers, residents of Tucker's birth place, and people of various ages and professions. They organise their activities with an enviable regularity, attend the museums that display Torpedoes, exchange gossip, or simply spend time together. It is possibly the only car club in which the cars in existence are so dramatically outnumbered by the membership. Only around 40 of the club's members are actual owners of the car. The remaining 500-plus just want to keep alive the legend of what they regard as one of the best cars ever made.

The story of Preston Tucker does indeed sound like a legend; yet it is true, as is his fullfilment of his dream of the ideal car.

Felix WANKEL

The life of the fanatical German engineer Felix Wankel was not an easy one. Even though he lived to see his idea materialise, his work was only appreciated posthumously.

Felix Wankel was born on 13 August, 1902, in Lahr, a region of Swabia. It is worth noting that almost all of the genius German inventors come from Swabia, including Gottlieb Daimler, Karl Benz, and Nikolaus Otto.

Felix's father, a forester, died during the First World War. Felix managed to finish only secondary school – the family was too short of money for further education, which was why all Felix's engineering knowledge had to be self-taught. After he finished school, he worked as an apprentice in a publishing house. Being a bookbinder didn't inspire him, though; he was more interested in the actual machines that were used in the publishing house. He always looked on with envy at the mechanics who repaired the large apparatus.

Aged 22, Felix became interested in the idea of rotary engines. This was a time when Germany was going through a depression, and the young man joined the

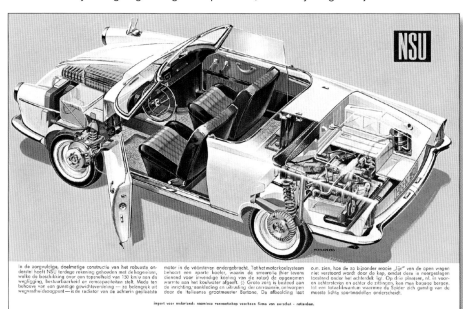

In de zorgvuldige, doelmatige constructie van het robuuste on- motor in de vóórsteven ondergebracht. Tot het motorkoelsysteem o.m. zien, hoe de zo bijzonder mooie „lijn" van de open wagen
derstel heeft NSU terdege rekening gehouden met de hoge eisen, behoort een aparte koeler, waarin de smeerolie (hier tevens niet verstoord wordt door de kap, omdat deze in neergeslagen
welke de beschikking over een topsnelheid van 150 km/u aan de dienend voor inwendige koeling van de rotor) de opgenomen toestand onder het achterdek ligt. Op drie plaatsen, nl. in voor-
wegligging, bestuurbaarheid en remcapaciteiten stelt. Mede ten warmte aan het koelwater afgeeft. ❄ Grote zorg is besteed aan en achtersteven en achter de zittingen, kan men bagage bergen,
behoeve van een gunstige gewichtsverdeling — zo belangrijk uit de inrichting, aankleding en uitrusting der carrosserie, ontworpen tot een totaal-kwantum waarmee de Spider zich gunstig van de
wegvastheidsoogpunt — is de radiator van de achterin geplaatste door de Italiaanse grootmeester Bertone. De afbeelding laat meeste lichte sportmodellen onderscheidt.

import voor nederlands naamloze vennootschap voorheen firma van oerschot - rotterdam.

An old sales brochure of the NSU Wankel Spider shows how little space the engine takes up. (Courtesy Phil Seed)

unemployed masses. While he didn't have anything better to do, he opened a small repairs shop in Heidelberg, but he didn't have a lot of customers because people were trying to save money and do as much DIY as possible.

Whiling away the time in his small and pitiful repair shop, Felix read many technical books and dreamt of a new type of engine – a powerful and economic one. Within two years, he had managed to develop the idea to the extent that he decided to take out a patent for his new invention. But the enthusiastic young man was disappointed to discover that a fellow countryman, Enke, had taken out a patent for a similar device 40 years prior to him. Felix came back to his repair shop, but he didn't give up – just the opposite, in fact. He set to work with an even greater fervour. In 1929, he got his first patent for a new type of rotary engine and a special gasket construction. Interestingly, it was the gaskets that had been the stumbling block for all the previous researchers of rotary engines. The problem wasn't resolved by Galloway – creator of the theoretical principle of rotary engine functioning – nor by any of his successors.

It was the 1930s, and, despite being a talented and skilful inventor, Felix Wankel was still in constant need of money, and often went hungry. The growing anger at capitalism drove Wankel into the circles of the National Socialists. New political convictions didn't bring him prosperity, but in one of the gatherings he met his wife. Both young activists were fortunately sensible enough to leave the National Socialist party at the right time. In 1933, events unfolded very quickly, and if he hadn't left the party for good, Felix Wankel would have found himself marching down a street in a brown shirt. Still, he had another problem – the Nazis now considered him a turncoat and threw him into jail. But thanks to some influential German engineers he knew, Felix was discharged on the basis of lack of evidence.

For the next few years, Felix Wankel spent his time constructing and improving his rotary engine. Over time, Wankel noticed more and more new ways of using his invention. He constructed a small stationary rotary engine to power water pumps and air compressors, but the Allied army stopped his research. The French didn't have the

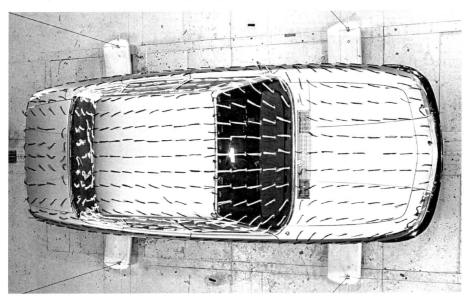

NSU RO80 was one of the first European cars to undergo proper aerodynamic testing. Attached to the car are airflow indicators. (Courtesy Phil Seed)

NSU RO80 displaying unusually advanced design features. (Courtesy Lothar Spurzem, under Creative Commons licence)

NSU RO80 – the sleek sideline. (Courtesy Lothar Spurzem, under Creative Commons licence)

time to sort out who was a fascist and who was not. Wankel's small repair shop was razed to the ground, along with any other suspicious factories in Heidelberg. Even this particular turn of events did not shock Wankel – he continued his work secretly, not admitting that he might have something else up his sleeve.

His efforts were eventually rewarded with the success he so richly deserved. In 1958, 34 long years since Wankel began his work, his rotary engine could be regarded as complete. His patience and determination was truly remarkable. It was possible to start the engine effortlessly; it hummed, rotated, and what's more important, it produced power. This cannot be said for any previous attempts to make a rotary engine. Wankel, wanting to protect himself from any nasty surprises, founded Wankel GmbH – a company that would look after his patents, and cash in the due payments from people using his ideas commercially.

Gradually, Felix Wankel waved good-bye to poverty, but proper recognition still evaded him. Even though 40,000 rotor cars were produced by NSU during his lifetime, the industry's big men reserved scornful sneers for Wankel and considered him an eccentric and an outsider. In his old age, he joined an animal welfare organization to fight for prohibition of scientific experiments on animals. In 1988, he died following a serious illness. Wankel had achieved much in his life, and experienced both despair and joy, but, amazingly, he never got his driving licence. Allegedly, he never drove an NSU, a Mazda or any other car. In reality, Dr Wankel had no interest in cars whatsoever.

RO80s survive in many different colour schemes.
(Courtesy Joachim Koehler, under GNU licence)

Some people thought that Wankel's invention had fallen into the abyss, but now it has been revived. The rotary engine is enjoying renewed popularity, thanks to the Mazda RX-8. Not only are the engines mass-produced by Mazda, but car enthusiasts and hot-rodders are reinventing this small, powerful, lightweight unit.

In 2003, the Mazda Renesis rotary engine received the title prize at the International Engine of the Year competition. The jury of car industry experts and journalists also named it the best new engine of the year, and best engine in category of 2.5 to 3-litre capacity. In the 2004 competition, the Renesis continued to dominate its category. It seems that the Japanese engineers have succeeded in breaking the old stereotype of rotary engines. A Renesis weighs only 260lb, while a piston engine of similar capacity is generally 100lb heavier. The Mazda Renesis is a light, powerful, and durable engine. It is compact and has an enviable power. The capacity of the Renesis is just 1.3 litres, but because of its power, it is taxed as a 2.6-litre engine. The original power output was 228bhp, but after turbocharging, it reaches 280bhp. The average fuel consumption is 30-34mpg, which is very good for such a powerful unit – high fuel consumption and incomplete combustion was a problem with the older rotary engines. Mazda has modified Wankel's construction to meet the USA's Clean Air Act, and the RX-8 is legal even in California, where laws for gas-guzzlers are especially strict.

The highly specific rotary engine has a promising future. Mazda has built a dual-fuel version of Wankel's engine that runs on petrol as well as hydrogen. Also, due to its low weight and small size, a rotary engine can be used in a hybrid electric car, where it is so important to keep assemby weight to a minimum.

Felix Wankel meets Kenichi Yamamoto – the man who we can thank for bringing the Wankel rotary engine concept back to life. (Courtesy Mazda)

Mazda RX8 – the most popular passenger car with a Wankel rotary engine. (Courtesy Rudolf Stricker, released under a GNU licence)

In 2002, Germany celebrated the 100th anniversary of Felix Wankel. It held a big event, with some of his former business partners and competitors attending. The convention saw cars and motorcycles that benefited from the fruits of the inventor: NSUs of the sixties, modern-day Mazdas, Citroen GS Bi-rotors, Mercedes-Benz C111s and Hercules, Suzukis, and Norton motorcycles. Everyone talked about the important invention Wankel had given the motoring world. However, during his lifetime, nobody was so generous as to just clap him on the shoulder and say: "Good job, man!"

Gabriel VOISIN

The Voisin brothers – Gabriel (left) and Charles. (Public domain image)

The greatest – possibly only – philosopher of the motor-era, Gabriel Voisin, was a man inclined towards perfection. The car, in his perception, was neither a means of transport nor a commodity. It wasn't a work of art either. The ideal car for Voisin was a materialisation of the design idea, a philosophical object whose sole reason for existence was logical distribution of all parts and an absolute harmony. Unlike the classic philosophers who were searching for the meaning of life, this refined Frenchman tried to find a totality of features that would make the car absolutely perfect. It is just possible that he may have succeeded, if factors such as money and power had not got in the way. He didn't manage to unfold his chain of philosophical connections completely; something remained unsaid. Although at one point he achieved financial success, he never cared how efficient his enterprise was. Always true to himself, he just wanted to get his message across. Yet acknowledgment of Voisin's indisputable genius came only after his death.

The car philosopher was born in 1880 in France. When his father left the family, his mother took both sons – Gabriel and Charles, who was two years younger – and moved to live with her father, a wonderful but very strict man. He brought up the two boys in a very regimented manner. The grandfather, who owned a small factory, indirectly encouraged Gabriel and Charles to turn their attention to engineering. They went to a prestigious school in Lyons, but took every opportunity to return to the provincial setting for some angling or open air expeditions. Later, Voisin would admit that his brother was his best friend.

A promotional postcard featuring the Voisin brothers. (Public domain image)

Although very young, they had already built a model airplane, a gun, and even a small car. The idea of flying was something that fascinated both young men most of all. Clement Ader, an ardent French engineer and visionary whom Gabriel met in 1900 while working at the Universal Exhibition in Paris, further aroused his interest in all things technical. Ader encouraged Voisin to experiment with aeronautics, and the brothers succeeded in building a functional aeroplane scale model. On 17 December 1903 the famous Wright brothers managed the world's first controlled flight and set a precedent for other budding aero-engineers to follow.

In 1906 Gabriel and Charles finally built an aeroplane that could take off and even remain airborne for a while. The same year the brothers founded the first airline in the world, earning the acclaim of their fellow Frenchmen. The airline also helped to improve their finances tremendously. Three years later, Gabriel became the youngest man to be made a Knight (lower rank) of the Legion d'Honneur order – he was only 29 years old. Tragically, in 1912 Charles died in a car crash. Gabriel continued the work they had both begun, but due to his brother's death he had lost his mental equilibrium, and his life would never be the same again.

During the First World War, Gabriel Voisin became the biggest aircraft supplier for the French army. After the war, having produced more than 10,000 aeroplanes, he didn't want to be involved in aviation any more. People close to Voisin said that he had left aviation because he couldn't deal with the fact that his aircraft would bring death to people.

Gabriel became involved with the automotive industry with a renewed vigour. His brother's death and the war had changed his perception of life profoundly. You couldn't really call him superstitious, but Gabriel saw a deeper meaning in even the little things in life. He used a similar approach for car production. Everything had its own sense, and everything was there for a reason. He didn't want to move too far from his aviation roots. Constructing his cars, he put to use everything that he had learnt while producing aeroplanes. At first glance this may have seemed odd, as a car and an

GABRIEL VOISON

A fighter plane built by Gabriel Voisin for the French WWI effort. (Public domain image)

aircraft are totally different things. But Gabriel Voisin wouldn't have agreed with this. A perfect car, in his opinion, should be manufactured with the same set of features as a perfect aeroplane. He wanted to adapt a car to have the six basic values of an aeroplane: lightness of construction, aerodynamics, perfect handling, safety, reliability, and economy.

However, from the marketing perspective, an aeroplane and a car are products that require a completely different approach. A car is generally produced to be in use for five years or so, but the working life of an aeroplane is longer – nobody would want to spend millions on an aircraft that would run out of 'steam' within a few years. Voisin couldn't bear the mindset of marketing, especially when it came to cars. He reasoned that if it was possible to make an aircraft that lasts for dozens of years, it must be possible to create a car that grows old with its owner, and even makes a good legacy for the owner's grandchild. Voisin would certainly be persona non grata today – the current consumer-producer relationship is based on a totally opposite principle, namely shortening the potential working life of an item to encourage a customer to buy again.

Voisin used the six aforementioned values of an aircraft like a roadmap when making his cars. He managed to achieve his goal. Even his first cars, although not as refined as his later work, were a symphony of design and technical imagination. They were fast, beautiful, relatively economic, safe, and extremely reliable. The only fault with Voisin's cars was the lack of real marketing vision. Voisin wouldn't listen to people talking about marketing – he had omitted the word from his vocabulary. His cars were not only the best, but also the most expensive in the world. Fortunately, the Europe of the 1920s wasn't short on celebrities and superstars, and these were the only people who could possibly afford a Voisin.

He popularised motoring ideas, taking an active part in the social life of France. Being blessed with a certain charm, he mixed in the upper circles of society, where he enjoyed undivided attention from the ladies and admiration from the gentlemen. At one of these social events he met the eccentric architect Le Corbusier. Both were nonconformist thinkers, even if their fields of art were so different, and they found common ground and influenced one another. Voisin shared his vision of the advantages of the functional city-building of the future, while Le Corbusier, in turn, made Voisin look at design from another angle. Both artists came to the conclusion that it wasn't possible to experiment with design without a reason. It would be foolish to do something just to surprise people, or toy with new, unprecedented shapes. Design should be integrated with functionality and ergonomics. In the later works of Voisin and Le Corbusier, it is actually possible to see many common features. A cosy car and a dynamic dwelling – it is a great idea.

Gabriel Voisin became acquainted with the car engineer André Citroën, who was ever-present at social occasions, and played the part of Don Juan more enthusiastically

*A blue 1927 Voisin C12 Tourer with a six-cylinder, 4.5-litre engine.
(Courtesy Le Riche Automobile Restorers CI Ltd, Jersey, leriche.com)*

than Voisin. In 1917, when all Voisin's thoughts were focused on building his own car, André Citroën had already acquired a certain popularity as an engineer. Knowing that Citroën was considering production of a small democratic vehicle, engineers and designers were streaming to the Maestro in the hope of finding jobs. Swindlers and flatterers were often among them. Artault and Dufresne, mediocre engineers who had just left Panhard & Levassor, wanted to sell Citroën some ideas acquired during their work at P&L. They offered a four-cylinder 16bhp engine, which they passed off as their own masterpiece. It wasn't a bad engine, but the fact was that the 'masterpiece' was largely copied from a prototype made at the Panhard & Levassor workshop.

André Citroën wanted something smaller and lighter. The prospective engine had a 3-litre capacity and it was too heavy for a small democratic car. To a certain extent, finances played a major part in this decision. André Citroën didn't have sufficient funds, but Artault and Dufresne wanted to make big money as quickly as possible.

Knowing that his friend took an interest in large engines, Citroën sent both engineers to Voisin. He took Artault and Dufresne on as part of his small team, and they began to work on a Grand Prix sports car. When his first car was almost completed, Artault and Dufresne disappeared from the scene. They reappeared at Peugeot's headquarters full of Voisin's ideas, which he hadn't had time to patent. Soon Peugeot overtook Voisin in the French Grand Prix, with the help of his own technology.

It is hard to blame Peugeot for plagiarism – it might not have known that the ideas weren't original. Voisin was shocked because he realised what had happened.

Gabriel Voisin (left) developed the philosophy of car design. (Courtesy Philippe Ladure, Les Amis de Gabriel Voisin, avions-voisin.org)

However, this misunderstanding didn't change the friendly relationship between Voisin and Citroën. Both were ardent defenders of the idea of an industrial society. They knew how society should develop, in order to make rapid progress, but they had no time to put their theories into practice. Artists and engineers in politics was surely not a good combination. More to the point, who would understand the free-thinking men, who asserted that, before the '60s, Western countries would become fully industrialised and manual toil would be removed, even from traditional practices such as agriculture? Apparently, Voisin and Citroën overestimated the ability of future generations. The level of progress they had anticipated has not yet been achieved, even in the 21st century. Manual work is still pretty much on our agenda, and will continue to be for the forseeable future.

André Citroën considered Henry Ford his idol. He even made his way to the USA to meet the famous inventor of the conveyor assembly line, and to share impressions with him. It appeared to Henry Ford that the Frenchman, with all those utopian ideas, was a little strange. However, he never spurned advice when it applied to mass production, or the strategy of car manufacturing. Voisin was more reserved towards Ford, as he thought him too mercenary and, as he made his cars only for money, they lacked personality and character.

Citroën and Voisin had very different ideas, and went their separate ways in the end. Citroën wanted to make small and cheap cars, but Voisin ... if he only had the technical opportunities, he would build a 30ft-long limo and equip it with a 32-cylinder engine. How, then, did he manage to influence the development of Citroën's cars and possibly the development of the French car industry? Ultimately, it was his extensive knowledge that made him a man to whom others looked up.

A much more productive collaboration was that between Voisin and André Lefebvre, whom he had transferred from his aircraft works to cars. The boss and the young man understood each other perfectly. They were totally lacking in any respect for accepted standards and for car building traditions. They sometimes even decided to construct something unusual and absurd, just to challenge their boredom. During the early '20s, Voisin cars remained unbeaten on the race tracks, reaching a peak with the 1922 hat trick, when three Voisin C3 cars finished in the top three positions at the Grand Prix of Automobile Club de France. All these brilliant victories would have been impossible without Lefebvre.

Voisin and Lefebvre worked together for 15 years. When Lefebvre left the 'Car lab' in 1931, he went on to work with Citroën. He made his teacher proud by implementing revolutionary ideas for the benefit of the French car industry. This time, Voisin had no objection to a protégé leaving his team for a 'competitor.' The first financial difficulties had started to creep in, and occasionally Voisin had had to make job cuts. That is not to say that he forced Lefebvre out, but he just knew that his own approach was too different from a large-scale production perspective. In later years, he felt happy looking at Citroën models, and seeing some of his utopian ideas going into the mainstream. Since 1933, Citroën, mainly thanks to Lefebvre and his excellent teacher, has held the status of the most innovative French car producer.

Even if Citroën wasn't the first man who made a front-wheel drive car, it was Lefebvre who, helped by Citroën, brought this layout to the masses. The Citroën Traction Avant was the first mass-produced car with front-wheel drive, and it inspired other engineers around the world.

Back to 1919 – the year Voisin founded his car works. His work began with a pomp, as he took to experimenting with large capacity engines – Voisin's plan was to build one with an 8-litre capacity. Thanks to huge capital investments, he managed it, but it was probably more suited to being part of a display in the Louvre. It was visually impressive and a genuine work of art, but too complicated, and it had more technical faults than advantages. It would hardly have been viable to produce that sort of engine. Voisin felt a little disappointed, but he didn't capitulate.

Voisin lowered the bar a little, but still didn't stray too far from his initial ideas. Both Citroën and Voisin had prepared very successful models. Citroën offered the Type-A – a small, cheap car with a 1.3-litre engine. Within a short time, he received thousands of orders, and in the two short years that the Type-A existed, it sold more than 24,000 units. Voisin, in turn, released the model C1, which – like the Type-A – was largely constructed by André Citroën. It had a huge engine, and unlike the Type-A, was meant for quite a different market sector. As a result, only 70 C1s were sold. Although it was just a drop in the ocean compared with Citroën's thousands, the futurist Voisin was happy. Car production didn't increase his wealth (the opposite, in fact) but he had finally found his real calling in life.

Voisin did very well in the 1920s. His social networking helped to build the right image. Rich men dreamt of ordering a car from Voisin. The highest point of the Voisin cars' popularity was the 1930s, when the fashionable Art Deco masterpieces Simoun and C28 appeared. Simoun was at the time considered the most beautiful car of the century. It was extraordinarily big and extraordinarily heavy. It is an almost unreal feeling to look at the Simoun, and realise that this huge work of art can actually move.

Many were of the opinion that the Simoun was Voisin's answer to the 1927 Bugatti Royale, which was created especially for royalty. Unfortunately, the kings and queens of Europe didn't seem to be impressed by either car. Although the Simoun is considered a work of art, it is a very impractical car. It was another attempt by Voisin to build a V12 sleeve valve engine, but he was not very impressed with the outcome as the engine only produced 113bhp. Although this didn't stop the car from clocking speeds over 90mph, the brake horsepower didn't give him much to be proud of. For example, a

Voisin C28 Aerosport 1935 – an unusually smooth and aerodynamic body for the '30s. (Courtesy Gilles Blanchet)

Duesenberg Model J of the same era had 265bhp at its disposal. But then Voisin had never worried too much about power and speed. Driveability and safety were more important for him.

One of the last Voisin masterpieces was the 1935 Aerodyne. The car had an absolutely radical appearance. It is now considered by historians as the first step in the direction of a pontoon-type body, the forerunner of today's typical car, where the wings do not protrude and the body has flat sides.

The winds of change could already be seen in the aforementioned Simoun. Unlike other cars of 1931, it had no running board at all. Voisin believed in the future of pontoon-type bodies. He asserted that in five years, all car designers would give up wings and running boards. At that time, there were people who laughed at Voisin's statements, but shortly after the Second World War, the majority of car designers suddenly learnt to really appreciate pontoon bodies. Elegant wings, running-boards, and forward protruding headlamps disappeared, making room for a more functional design – just like Voisin had predicted.

In 1936, Voisin lost control of his enterprise. As much as he hated the word 'marketing,' he should have realised that only a businessman who knew how to manage money efficiently, and invest funds reasonably, could remain in the car business. Voisin was never too bothered about money, and he spent it easily. He was generous with his friends and with himself, and he was ready to pour any sum of money into car construction. He wanted to realise the basic postulates of his philosophy through technology, but the only flaw was that people couldn't pay for his ideas. Although his cars were very expensive as new, in the early '60s, it was possible to pick up a used Voisin for as little as $500-$1000. However, as fashion and perception have changed, antique Voisins are once again amongst the most expensive cars in the world. After his death, Voisin was nicknamed 'Don Quixote' by a journalist. Don Quixote's battle with a windmill is symbolic of taking on an unsurpassable obstacle.

C30 Dubos 1938 – one of Voisin's last cars. (Courtesy Gilles Blanchet)

Until the 1960s, Voisin took an active part in the social life of France, and was an advisor for many car engineers and designers. Together with his Spanish colleagues, he constructed an unconventional two-seater scooter car. He retired from the automotive scene at the age of 80, and settled in the quiet town of Tournus, where he devoted himself to writing. In 1965, the French government made him a Commander of the Legion d'Honneur. That was the second time he received the order, only this time he jumped two degrees higher. The genius Frenchman lived a rich and adventurous life, and reached a great age: he died in his home, in 1973, at the age of 93.

Knighthood and Maestro-status notwithstanding, we have still barely scratched the surface of Voisin's philosophy. The biggest part of his heritage is out of reach for the industrialists, and not only because of stubbornness or a lack of vision – money and efficiency are inescapable obstacles that determine the direction of the design, and the necessity of making a car functional whilst not compromising its aesthetic value is an ambition that has never been fulfilled. The search goes on ...

CARL BORGWARD

Carl Friedrich Wilhelm Borgward, one of the most talented German engineers, was born in 1890 in Altona, a small town near Hamburg. In the 19th century, Altona was an important harbour town on the river Elba, but people still lived in poverty. Carl's father was a coalman and his family led a hard existence. The father had to support 13 children, and Carl was the youngest of them. In Altona, only a few people had cars, but nearby Hamburg was full of 'steel horses' and Carl became fond of those noisy monsters.

Carl was determined not to follow in his father's footsteps. Continuing his gloomy and unprofitable business wasn't an option. Carl dreamt of receiving a technical education and owning a car factory. In his boyhood, he couldn't walk past any mechanical object without sitting down and tinkering with it. Whether it was a rusty clock or an old harvester, he had to explore it and repair it. Nobody had taught him to do it.

His family had little money, but his father scrimped and saved to send the talented young man to the Hoheren Machinenbauschule in Hamburg, where he studied mechanical engineering. In 1913, Carl Borgward obtained an engineering diploma and found his first job at Eilers Steel in Hanover. Soon he found an engineering position in Berlin and, despite his young age, received a similar salary to an experienced engineer. His dream had almost come true, at least one part of it, but the world suddenly changed when the First World War began. Borgward went to fight in 1915, fought bravely and was injured, but returned home safely.

He decided to move to Bremen, a beautiful city that could open up a wealth of possibilities to a technically-minded young man. But he miscalculated the odds – the depressed and war-stricken city didn't need Carl's innovative ideas. Making his living with casual work, he got introduced into certain business circles and became a partner of the businessman Ernst Baerold, with whom he began producing radiators, mudguards, and other parts for cars. Soon all of Bremen took notice of Carl's activity, especially the Hansa-Lloyd Werke car plant. He received a large order to make radiators, but it really wasn't what he felt to be his purpose in life. The talented engineer didn't give up hope of producing his own cars, despite the postwar circumstances.

Carl had to start with something small and original. The idea of producing a small lorry for small and middle-sized businesses was positively received. Germany had just suffered a wave of inflation, and many car plants had gone bankrupt. Borgward had only 60 employees at his disposal – these days, it would be almost unthinkable to venture into the lorry business with such a small staff. Today, one of the most famous lorry producers, Scania, employs more than 25,000 workers. Still, Borgward succeeded in making one of the most popular European commercial cars of the '20s. You could hardly call it a lorry, but it was the content that mattered.

The engineer called his masterpiece 'a wheelbarrow.' This amusing, three-wheeled vehicle was equipped with a 1200cm³ DKW engine and could shift a 550lb load. The

A single-cylinder Goliath Pioneer.
(Courtesy Norman Williams, Borgward Drivers Club, borgward.org.uk)

official name of the vehicle was the Blitzkarren, which meant 'lightning wheelbarrow.' The name didn't really reflect its dynamic properties – Blitzkaren was slow, but very practical and cheap to run.

Borgward's wheelbarrow cost only 980 marks, while compact lorries from his competitors cost 3000 to 5000 marks. Small shop owners and delivery workers were over the moon. From 1924, six units of Blitzkarren rolled down Borgward's conveyor every day. In the beginning, Borgward did everything himself – he was the generator of ideas, bookkeeper, cleaner, and distributor. The talented engineer drove around Germany at the wheel of his Blitzkarren and showed off his vehicle to potential buyers.

Borgward's original and outgoing approach soon began to bear fruit. With the help of shipbuilder Wilhelm Tecklenburg, he managed to sell a lot of wheelbarrows to the postal service. That was the best imaginable publicity for his miniature lorries. Borgward soon rebuilt the wheelbarrow, and renamed it – amusingly – the Goliath Rapid. Now all three wheels were equipped with brakes (the first model had brakes on the rear wheels only), the car had a starter, a clutch, and could go into reverse at last. The loading capacity increased to 1300lb, but the price went up by only a fraction to 1100 marks. The volume of production grew day by day, and was now measured in thousands. By 1928, Borgward had 300 employees. Germany and the rest of Europe had recovered from the consequences of war and business was once again booming. However, 1929 brought new troubles – the world faced a financial crisis. Borgward was largely unaffected by the crisis because cheap commercial cars were still popular, but other car producers in Germany weren't so lucky.

When the famous Hansa-Lloyd enterprise went to rack and ruin, Borgward didn't think twice – this was his big chance. He and Tecklenburg took over the Hansa-Lloyd plants. The government agreed to give them the enterprise for free, on the condition that both partners would accept the entire debt of Hansa-Lloyd. Borgward decided to temporarily interrupt the current production of passenger vehicles that went on at Hansa and continue with medium-weight lorries and commercial vehicles. It is incredible to think about the low expectations of small businesses at that time, but Borgward had investigated the market in detail. He only made vehicles that were in

The Goliath Pioneer was simple and practical.
(Courtesy Norman Williams, Borgward Drivers Club)

The Goliath Lorry – an affordable vehicle for a small business owner.
(Courtesy Norman Williams, Borgward Drivers Club)

demand, cheap but good quality. Nowadays, the mere thought of a three-wheeled lorry with the body made of tarpaulin would give you the shivers, but during the financial crisis of the '30s it was very popular, and small shop owners praised Borgward for his effort. The small lorry was tax exempt and could be driven without a licence.

Before long, passenger cars appeared on the production lines of Hansa-Lloyd. The 1932 Goliath Pioneer was a simple, light vehicle on three wheels. The tiny two-seater was powered by a single-cylinder 200cc engine. Thanks to the tarpaulin bodywork, it weighed only a few hundred pounds and cost 1400 marks. Although this car was very basic, Borgward managed to sell 4000 units in three years.

1959 Goliath 'Goli' – Borgward's three-wheel lorries enjoyed a steady demand all through his career. (Courtesy Norman Williams, Borgward Drivers Club)

The National Socialist government began to popularise motorisation – Hitler had said that each German family should have at least one car. In 1934, Borgward realized his dream and started to produce cars; and this time, they were real cars. The Hansa 400 and Hansa 500 soon appeared on the market. Even though Borgward now made his car using predominantly steel, some parts were still made from tarpaulin. He hoped that these new four-seaters would further the motorisation of Germany and make his company an important player in the country's car industry, but it didn't happen – the small cars came a little too late. The financial crisis was over, and people turned their attention towards bigger and more beautiful cars. Some people poked fun at Borgward's models, and newspapers published cartoons. "Dogs bark but the caravan moves on," read one of the captions, referring to the old Arabic proverb about a person who continues with his endeavour, despite public opinion. Nevertheless, the government became interested in Borgward's enterprise and ordered a batch of military vehicles. The National Socialists were obviously preparing for war, without people realising that this was the case.

Even though the experienced engineer was yet to achieve success in the passenger car business, he had much to be proud of: in the mid-1930s, his company was the biggest lorry producer in Germany. Adapting swiftly to market requirements, Borgward made a car that was, in his opinion, ideal for a middle class German. This time he hit the nail on the head – the Hansa 1100 received great acclaim. It was a full-bodied car, no tarpaulin, all in cold steel. The handsome sedan with a dynamic four-cylinder engine proved popular. It cost 2750 marks and was a direct competitor to the Opel 1.3-litre. Both cars cost the same – it was image that decided the outcome. Borgward's car looked more expensive than it really was. Technically, the Hansa 1100 was somewhat better than the Opel. Borgward's 1.1-litre engine was 28bhp and the car's top speed was 59mph; fuel consumption was 31mpg. The Opel, regardless of a higher capacity, could squeeze out only 24bhp. Its top speed was 56mph and fuel consumption was 28mpg.

Hansa 1700 Sport. (Courtesy Norman Williams, Borgward Drivers Club)

Hansa 1100 with a rare cabriolimousine body type.
(Courtesy Norman Williams, Borgward Drivers Club)

In total, Borgward produced 20,000 units of the Hansa 1100 before 1940. Opel's democratic car sold more due to better brand awareness – 29,000 units in the same period of time, regardless of worse technical specifications and a higher price (in 1936 the Opel 1.3 was already 200 marks more expensive than the Hansa 1100).

Further advancing his model range, Borgward designed two six-cylinder cars: the Hansa 1700 and Hansa 2000. In the late thirties, the relationship between Borgward and Tecklenburg began to fall apart as it became more and more difficult for them to find common ground. If truth be told, Tecklenburg was sick and tired of car production, whereas Borgward loved it more and more every day. As a car manufacturer, he was in his element, and was keen to get rid of the ever-grumpy Tecklenburg. Carl Borgward bought the shares from his former partner and both men walked away from the deal breathing freely. At last, Borgward could fulfil another dream of his: each car that rolled out of the Hansa plant now had the big, showy chromium-plated name of Borgward on the grille.

Borgward was too immersed in his thoughts of mechanics and cars to notice that Germany had reached the brink of a great political change. In 1937, Borgward's native town Altona disappeared from the map – it was merged with Hamburg, which had spread out in all directions; Altona had now become its suburb. In 1940, Borgward already employed more than 8000 workers in this area.

Bremen was one of the cities that were ruthlessly destroyed by air-raids in the Second World War. Bombing devastated the main parts of the area, including Borgward's pride and joy, his factory. In 1945, three quarters of his facilities were destroyed by bombers.

After the war, it took a couple of years for the Allies to loosen their grip on German industry and allow the manufacturers to continue business as before. Borgward immediately found a way to deceive the Allies, who still controlled the delivery of raw materials. He registered three different companies – Borgward, Lloyd and Goliath. In reality they were the same enterprise, but now it received three times more material than before.

Work on a new passenger car began immediately, and in 1949, the Borgward Hansa 1500 became the first all-new German postwar car. Borgward had managed to outdo all his competitors. People named it the Beauty of Bremen, so modern and extraordinary was this vehicle. Compared to the old-fashioned Opel and Mercedes models, it looked irresistible. Borgward had actually constructed the car almost by himself – despite the fact that more than 1000 people were working with him after the war, he still continued to be a one-man orchestra, even designing the cars himself.

Thanks to this unprecedented success, both employees and competitors now referred to the talented engineer as Dr Borgward. In 1949, he went back to his old ways and designed a new three-wheel lorry, the Goliath 750. This time, there was no

Lloyd LT 600, one of the world's first minivans, entered production in 1954. (Courtesy Norman Williams, Borgward Drivers Club)

CARL BORGWARD

Lloyd LP 300 Leukoplastbomber – this little tarpaulin car played a pivotal role in the motorisation of postwar Germany.
(Courtesy Norman Williams, Borgward Drivers Club)

irony and no cartoons in the newspapers – Germany again needed a cheap and simple commercial vehicle. Borgward remembered the mockery of the Hansa 400 and 500 models, but there was no time to look back. This mockery didn't stop him toying with the idea of a tarpaulin car once again.

In 1950, the Lloyd LP300 came out on the market – the car had a wooden frame covered with tarpaulin. Germans named it the Leukoplastbomber, or plaster bomber. In seven years, 45,000 units were sold. The car was unbelievably light and simple. Its small two-stroke engine produced only 10bhp, but this was enough for it to pick up a maximum speed of 43mph. It was remarkable that Carl Borgward had the ability to catch the vibe of the market and sometimes even predict the shift in demand. His company went from making simple, cheap cars to making the most popular, luxury cars in Germany within just a few short years.

In 1954, Borgward reached the pinnacle of his fame. The model Isabella was ready – design-wise, it went along the same lines of the Hansa 1500, but was more slender, modern, and technically perfect.

"Cars from Bremen – cars with an excellent reputation" was the advertising pitch that Borgward came up with to popularise his new car. It wasn't just an empty slogan – the Isabella really was a car with an excellent reputation. Mercedes, Porsche and BMW were really unhappy that Borgward had this sort of success. The big companies spent millions making cars that weren't always successful. Meanwhile, the doctor from Bremen who didn't have their millions had been able to produce a new model on his own, and his work was always better quality. Borgward was a perfectionist; he turned his attention to the smallest details. That was the real reason why the cars from Bremen had an excellent reputation. Borgward couldn't bear it when things didn't move as quickly as he'd like them to. When he saw an employee working without enthusiasm,

Borgward Hansa 1500 – one of the earliest pontoon car bodies in the world. Pictured is a very early version with no direction indicators on the wings. (Courtesy Norman Williams, Borgward Drivers Club)

Borgward Hansa 1500 after a face-lift, with more elegant mirrors and streamline direction indicators on the wings. (Courtesy Norman Williams, Borgward Drivers Club)

he used to say "Keep my advanced age in mind – you're spending so long messing about that I might not live to see the result."

Borgward's empire spread quickly, with passenger cars, tricycles, lorries, ship engines and even a helicopter on the drawing board. While BMW was on the verge of ruin, Borgward celebrated the 500,000th car since the money reform in 1948. Borgward

Borgward 511 – the four-wheel lorries were as popular as the three-wheel models. (Courtesy Norman Williams, Borgward Drivers Club)

couldn't compete with giants like Opel and Mercedes – they had the backing of huge capital. But Borgward never aimed to make a big profit. His only wish was to produce good quality, beautiful cars. This man was very humane and soft-hearted by nature, and he did his best to make the world a better place. Borgward never shouted at his employees. When the boss said: "Attention, my cigar has gone out!" then they all knew that he was annoyed and tried not to get in his way.

Unfortunately, it is very difficult to remain in big business with a humane approach such as this. Idealists, as it usually happens, fly too close to the sun and live in a world of their own. In the mid-fifties, Borgward had the chance to take over the BMW company. Such a move would have secured the future of Borgward's enterprise, but he couldn't even entertain such a possibility as it would have meant getting rid of most of the staff, and he didn't like the idea of depriving people of their jobs. A few years later, if the allegations are true, BMW would stick the knife into its competitor's back without even stopping to consider what was right or wrong.

In 1956, Borgward increased his capacity to 108,000 cars a year. Experts anticipated that Borgward, together with Volkswagen, would become the supermagnates of the German car industry. The model line of the Isabella offered more variety now: besides the standard sedan, a beautiful sports coupé and a pick-up were also produced. In 1959, visitors to the Brussels car show saw what would become the final model of Borgward – an exclusive limo P100. It replaced the Hansa 2400, which was considered one of the most beautiful postwar cars in Germany. The P100 went onto the production line, but its life was short. Only 2547 units were built. It was equipped with pneumatic suspension, and after a few years Mercedes would do the same, declaring its model to be the first German car with such a feature.

The sports car Arabella, in contrast to Borgward's other models, was a failure. He believed in the success of this car, but it just wasn't to be. Various technical faults haunted it, and people were reluctant to buy it. It is understandable that no car enterprise can only ever have successful models. Everybody makes mistakes. On the

Hansa 2300 Pullman limousine. (Courtesy Norman Williams, Borgward Drivers Club)

Borgward 2400 of the late '50s, sporting a superb fastback body.
(Courtesy Norman Williams, Borgward Drivers Club)

other hand, there are car manufacturers whose entire model history is one big mess, but some of them continue to produce cars. I will not name any names; the most knowledgeable car fans will understand what I am talking about.

In spite of the failure of the Arabella, Borgward continued to flourish and develop. The amount of exports increased considerably – his cars were appreciated all around

Borgward 1500 Sportcoupé, nicknamed 'Rennsport,' 1954, was aimed at the younger buyer. (Courtesy Norman Williams, Borgward Drivers Club)

Carl Borgward working on a scale model of one of his prototypes. (Courtesy Borgward Automotive)

the world, even in New Zealand and Australia. In fact, at one time, only 36.5 per cent of his production (including lorries and engines) were sold in Germany, with everything else sold abroad.

In 1960, the financial instability that had set in meant that Borgward's export prospects narrowed. The home trade didn't do as well as before, either. If truth be told, Borgward's enterprise was still run on prewar managerial principles – it had a strong leader and a large amount of less important employees. Carl Borgward was an engineer, not a planner, but thanks to his perfect intuition, he knew what was right and may have been able to keep afloat for quite a long time. Unfortunately, a plot was brewing amongst Bremen's politicians and big car producers. Their goal was to ruin Borgward's empire.

In the winter of 1960-1961, the German car industry ran into problems. Experts thought that this wouldn't be an ongoing thing, and eventually they were proved right. Borgward looked at the possibility of getting a loan to pass this unsuccessful spell. In a period of stagnation, it is normal to take out a loan to keep up the flow of money because it allows businesses to buy materials and keep production going as normal. Strangely, all the Bremen banks he approached refused him, even with Borgward's spotless reputation. The news about Borgward looking for a loan spread to the media, and the newspaper Bild managed to cast a slur on his good name. Even though Bild had been known to publish unverified information and rumours, it was a popular paper. It is alleged that people from the BMW company spread rumours about Borgward's bankruptcy, and the Bild was happy to publish the 'news.'

Isabella was Carl Borgward's biggest success – more than 200,000 were made. (Courtesy Norman Williams, Borgward Drivers Club)

Car enthusiasts' favourite – an Isabella Cabriolet. (Courtesy Norman Williams, Borgward Drivers Club)

Hard-top Isabellas lined up. (Courtesy Norman Williams, Borgward Drivers Club)

CARL BORGWARD

The information about Borgward's financial position was false – he was not threatened by bankruptcy. Bremen's council joined in this unfair strategy, and demanded that he sign the renunciation of his enterprise. When he refused, some officials found another way of getting their hands on his company.

Borgward was invited to a meeting to revise the matter of his company's solvency. The meeting began early in the morning, and continued until half past eleven at night. All day long, the officials dissected Borgward and his financial documents, doing their best to prove the insolvency of his firm. The meeting ended with Borgward signing the renunciation of control of his enterprise. The 70-year-old engineer gave in to the pressure as he couldn't think straight at the end of the day. The council of Bremen had triumphed, and Borgward Motorwerke went into administration.

One part of the administrator's duties was settling accounts with creditors. And who was this administrator? Johannes Semmler, a German politician and co-founder of the Christian Social Union in Bavaria. He became president of the advisory board of BMW in 1960, when BMW was struggling and facing bankruptcy. At the same time, he was selected by the Bremen council as the consultant and head of the Borgward advisory board. It has been suggested that he settled an interesting fee for himself and some other nice benefits for his secretary, including a very beautiful Isabella car.

Four years after the liquidation procedure, it emerged that Borgward had had sufficient money, and was capable of settling accounts with his deliverers and other creditors with a million to spare. Of course, it was too late to do anything then. The leftover cash went into Bremen's budget, and after a while it is rumoured to have reappeared at the BMW motor plant in the form of a subsidy.

Bremen's council annihilated Carl Borgward's life's work and took his money. 23,000 employees were dismissed, and in 1962 an unemployment crisis began in the Bremen region – no wonder, considering 20 per cent of the population involved in heavy industry worked at Borgward Motorwerke. Those people were turned away, the motor plant was partly dismantled and sold; all unfinished cars and helicopters went to the scrap heap. Borgward couldn't stand looking at the ruin of his life's achievement. He suffered a serious heart attack and died on 28 July, 1963. It's strange that Borgward had to fight the battle all by himself: what happened to his friends and partners?

Not only beautiful but also practical – an Isabella Kombi with a universal-type body.
(Courtesy Norman Williams, Borgward Drivers Club)

73

P100 Limousine – Carl Borgward's personal favourite, and the last car built before the shameful plot. (Courtesy Norman Williams, Borgward Drivers Club)

Military vehicles were also on Borgward's agenda.
(Courtesy Norman Williams, Borgward Drivers Club)

Mexican entrepreneurs bought all the production lines and the right to use the Borgward trademark, hoping to start large-scale car production in their country. However, the bureaucracy and stubbornness of the Mexican government created obstacles for their plans. Four long years passed before they received permission to set up production lines and begin manufacturing. Mexico continued to produce the Isabella and the P100 until 1970, making a total of 2267 cars. In Mexico, Brazil, and even South Africa you can still catch a glimpse of an old Mexican-made Borgward. The empty Borgward works in Bremen were used by Hanomag to produce its buses.

It is difficult to understand how such a huge motor plant could disappear from the chapters of car history books. The world has forgotten about the fourth biggest

German car maker and the genius engineer that stood at its helm. Even the Germans themselves don't exactly know who Carl Borgward was. However, it is more than possible that this is about to change. Christian – Carl Borgward's grandson, who only knows of his magnificent grandfather from his father's stories and from press comments – plans to continue the family tradition. At the time of writing he is not ready to show his hand, and the particulars of his new automobile remain under wraps, but Christian is convinced that the car could lure many people away from Mercedes and Porsche.

While the work on the new car is in full swing, I can offer you an exclusive interview with the man who will bring the Borgward name into the sunshine again.

Arvid Linde: Do you know which of his cars was your grandfather's favourite?

Christian Borgward: His favourite car was a Borgward P100 (dark grey colour).

AL: Considering the secrecy, what can you tell me about the new Borgward car? Do you have any technical specifications available for publishing?

CB: The new Borgward cars are totally independent developments. Due to the fact that we aim to shift the paradigm in the industry, we have been analysing the actual and future automotive concepts and platforms. Keeping in mind our heritage and the ideas and genius my grandfather and also my father stand for, it was quite clear that we must focus on complete independence. We have to achieve our brand values of innovation, intelligence, efficiency, reliability, quality, profitability, elegance, and style.

We have created a flexible platform, new powertrain concepts, and some very innovative technical solutions in the field of materials and functions. According to the Borgward Heritage, our cars will be positioned in the premium segment and will have to meet the customer's requirements and expectations. We are convinced that there is a target group of Borgward customers who will appreciate our products as unique vehicles with a certain intelligent and out-of-the-box approach.

AL: How did you come into the car business? Was it a childhood passion or were you inspired by your grandfather?

CB: Unfortunately, and I am very sad about this, I did not grow up with my grandfather, due to the fact he died in 1963 and I was born in 1966. So my inspiration comes from my father, Claus Borgward. He was a great car enthusiast because of his father. He has been a very successful engineer with Volkswagen. He was the youngest member of the board of management of Volkswagen AG, responsible for quality.

My father told me a lot about the ideas of my grandfather, the way he built up his companies and how he involved and empowered his employees. His passion for cars and everything on wheels definitely motivated by my father. We drove a lot of different cars together and talked a lot about technical issues. Today, I am sure that I have been

given the unique opportunity to be inspired by the 'Borgward Gene.' It sounds funny but seems to be true. My grandfather inspired my father and me. My respect for both is what motivates me in my daily business, and in the progress of the revival of Borgward cars.

Christian Borgward.
(Courtesy Borgward Automotive)

How a Borgward car of the 21st century might look ...
(Courtesy Borgward Automotive, borgward-automotive.com)

AL: With the current climate of the global car industry, do you think you can find the gap in the market?

CB: Yes. My grandfather had to start again after the Second World War. There have always been tough times and environments. But there is room enough for good ideas, a strong heritage and the last independent German Premium car brand, if you work hard and are serious enough about it."

AL: Many people work on green car concepts now. Do you have any plans of developing a hybrid or electric car?

CB: As mentioned, we aim to achieve the requirements of our target customers and to deliver the brand values. Borgward always has been one of the innovative car manufactures ahead of competition, even at these times of powertrain technologies. When we started our development, future powertrain concepts have been the main focus. We will not ignore the reality in terms of hybrid or electric powertrain technology, I can assure you. Borgward will stick to this heritage even within the field of powertrain ideas.

AL: Can you tell me more about the Think Tank? When will that come about and how can one participate?

CB: This is a very innovative and unique idea for the industry. Borgward invites engineers and developers to become exclusive members of the Borgward-TechnologyThinkTank (B3T). It will be the forum where engineers, designers, specialists and scientist of related disciplines work together in the development of the future Borgward cars. By starting the B3T, Borgward sets a new milestone in the history of development of cars in the automotive industry and the revival of Borgward vehicles.

B3T members will be selected by Borgward AG and become a part of the international development team. Due to the fact that we work together based on the Borgward developments, the community will be very exclusive. It will be a group of developers who have to invest in the work and will receive a tremendous return-on-invest.

B3T members will meet twice a year in a convention to discuss and present the actual state of developments. To avoid any misuse or fraud of the secrecy and trust within this exclusive community, we will ask for an annual protective charge from each member. B3T members will receive an exclusive access to the community to exchange, discuss ideas and solutions on a permanent level.

AL: When do you plan to start producing the new car?

CB: When we are ready. Our plans are on track.

So, for the time being, we will just have to be patient and wait for the new Borgward car ...

Gerald WIEGERT

Gerald Wiegert's lifelong dream was to build a 100 per cent American supercar that would be more than a match for any of the Italian performance cars. Being a proud patriot, he wanted to make a car that would be built in the USA, using locally sourced materials, and technologies without any foreign influence. He approached this task very seriously and it seemed as if he was trying to completely re-invent the car.

Gerald Wiegert graduated with a Bachelor of Science degree in advanced vehicle design after five years of full tuition scholarship with distinction from both the Art Centre College of Design and the Centre for Creative Studies. He continued his education at four different US colleges, including one that specialised in advanced aircraft design. After working for numerous companies and clients, including Chrysler, Ford, General Motors Technical Centre, and as a personal consultant to the president of Toyota Motors, when he graduated from college, he decided to start his own company called Vehicle Design Force. His first prototype, named 'the Vector,' was projected to be sold at $100,000 retail in early 1970. The car was a design study that was featured at the LA Auto Expo and on the cover of *Motor Trend* magazine. This first Vector never went into production, but Wiegert came out of the project with more experience and know-how. He founded a new car company called Vector Aeromotive (with a reference to aircraft, because his childhood dream was to fly military jet fighters), and created a Vector W2 twin turbo supercar prototype. It had a tuned twin-turbo V8 engine based on an aftermarket sprint car aluminium small-block Chevrolet engine, producing over 600bhp. The maximum speed was estimated at 240mph, which, considering the power, was quite possible. But the W2 never left the prototype stage – being a perfectionist, Wiegert wasn't completely satisfied with the car. In the late '70s, foreign investors became interested in Wiegert's activities, but he stuck to his guns and decided to keep the Vector W2 an American car.

Soon he embarked on the W2 evolution project, code-named W8, which he approached as a commercial endeavour. He rebuilt a race-engineered Vector engine to suit his needs. It was worth the many sleepless nights – Wiegert's 6-litre engine was equipped with two turbochargers with intercoolers, and the maximum power of this V8 unit was 635bhp, with a whopping 854Nm torque.

In comparison with the popular import Lamborghini Countach, Wiegert had overtaken the Italians by far. Lamborghini's engine, although a V12, had only 374bhp and 362Nm torque. Porsche, Ferrari and other European brands were hardly any better, with no serious horsepower comparable to the Vector.

In the early nineties, after two pre-production prototypes and extensive testing, the Vector W8 was ready to go into production. Technologically, the W8 was far more advanced than the W2. The chassis for both cars was personally designed by Wiegert, and the construction was inspired by NASA and the US Air Force fighter aircraft. Electronic equipment and brakes also showed evidence of military substance and experience. One of Wiegert's staff had actually worked at the Pentagon, and

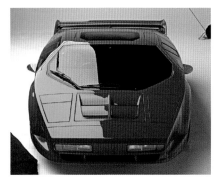

The Vector W8 – have they forgotten to add wings?
(Courtesy Vector Motors Corporation, vectormotors.com)

Advanced design, sophisticated technology, and the best available materials – it is a very rare supercar, as only 18 were made.
(Courtesy Vector Motors Corporation)

knew his way around military gadgetry. The Vector W8 had the most expensive car body in history – it was made of the best aerospace grade uni-directional high-quality composites. The body was very light and durable. From a manufacturing perspective, its only fault was the cost to build, which was in excess of any other automobile at the time. However, Wiegert had a uncompromising attitude for the Vector, and everything had to be the best. Vectors were the stars of virtually every show they attended around the world. Almost every kid on the planet had a Vector poster, and their cult following was huge.

Despite the price tag of $400,000, the orders started rolling in. Wiegert and his team had managed to successfully build 18 Vector W8s by hand, and they were sold to very wealthy individuals. The collector's exotic car market crashed in the early 1990s, but this did not seem to worry Wiegert too much. He already had a new Vector car on his drawing board.

The next stage of evolution of Wiegert's supercars, the Vector Avtech WX-3, was shown at the Geneva Auto Show in 1992 and 1993. Both visually and technically advanced, the WX-3 now featured a roadster alongside the aero-designed coupé with a 1250+hp engine, which eclipsed anything else at the time. The 7-litre monster allowed the car to reach a maximum speed of 270mph. The car went from zero to 60mph in 3.0 seconds – a 0.7-second improvement on W8. The unbelievable top speed meant that the Lockheed race engineered braking system was chosen to do the job. All four wheels were equipped with ventilated 13in brakes and 18in modular speedline wheels with Michelin tyres (the Lamborghini Countach only had 10in discs).

The WX-3 was almost a perfect car, and even better than the W8. Visually, it incorporated unique parallels with aircraft industry that could be seen all over. The side sub-windows were just like those of a military helicopter. But perfection cost money – it was estimated that the car would sell for $765,000. Although the price may have

An evolution of W8; the aviation theme develops further with Avtech WX-3, and the side sub-windows put you in mind of a fighter helicopter. 'Jetbike' water motorcycles are in the background. (Courtesy Vector Motors Corporation)

sounded high, the WX-3 was probably the best supercar available in the whole world at the time. And surely, the orders would roll in? Not quite …

On his return from Geneva, Wiegert received a nasty surprise. He found out that during his absence, his controlling interest in his enterprise was being undermined by an Indonesian company called Megatech. It had cheated Wiegert and his shareholders out of the purchase of Lamborghini by going behind Wiegert's back, after he masterminded the deal to buy Lamborghini from Chrysler. They stole the opportunity for themselves, and now planned to pool the Italian-American know-how into one company and dominate the supercar world. Although it is still a mystery exactly how the company slipped away from him, Wiegert did manage to protect all the intellectual property and patents to make sure Megatech could never legally produce any of his aerospace built cars. Wiegert was fired from his own company and for a while everything was being handled by the courts. Wiegert seemingly disappeared from the automotive 'stage' to prepare for a battle against the hostile takeover. He was also developing a new generation of flying boats (the Aquajet Corporation 'Jetbike' was a new Wiegert invention) and a new sports motorcycle, or superbike, for the water.

Scraping together the parts of the Vector's technology which had not been protected by copyright, and adding a Lamborghini V12 engine, the parasitic Megatech created a counterfeit, impostor Vector – the Vector M12. This is how Vector's badge went from symbolising some of the very best cars ever made – the W8 and the WX-3 – to one of the worst. The basic design of the car was based on the original WX-3, which, claims Wiegert, Megatech damaged by making unauthorised design changes. Although relatively cheap – the M12 cost less than $200,000 – only a few were made. The quality of assembly was poor or appalling, and interior details rattled at high speeds. Some automotive journalists tore the car to pieces, and the next 'cheap' Vector was even cheaper and even lower quality.

In the mid to late '90s the Indonesians fled from civil unrest against the Suharto dictatorship, and the remains of the once magnificent Vector Company were left to undeserving Indonesian cronies, calling themselves American Dream Aeromotive. Wiegert jumped in again by winning the court war, beating the people who fraudulently stole the company from him in a hostile takeover when they bribed a couple of directors. He regained control of what was left of his life's work, and renamed the company Vector Motors Corporation. Almost ten years had passed; time flies when you're having fun, according to Wiegert. Despite a couple of prototypes and an estimated 25 supercars sold during the '80s and '90s, Vector Motors is yet to create a production vehicle, except for prototypes – but it will. Extraordinary innovators and leaders like Wiegert always bounce back.

Display of power – Gerald Wiegert and the engines whose power output is yet to be matched by any other supercar. (Courtesy Vector Motors Corporation)

A glimpse of a full size WX-8 model. To bring this hypercar to fruition, serious investors are needed. (Courtesy Vector Motors Corporation, vectormotors.com)

Fellow Americans think highly of Gerald Wiegert – he was the creator of their first true supercar, as everything before the Vector was either a performance sports car, or an exotic. Wiegert singlehandedly raised the bar, and it has taken other companies almost 15 years to catch up. The innovations that Wiegert pioneered are numerous, including sequential shifting, heads-up displays, aerospace technology for cars, navigation systems, and twin-turbo charging, amongst others. In addition, the power output record for streetcars set by WX-3 still remains unbeaten. As far as the supercars

Gerald Wiegert: in the background, his latest creation – the WX-8.
(Courtesy Vector Motors Corporation)

go, you would struggle to find anyone more knowledgeable than Wiegert. He has acted as an independent advanced vehicle designer and consultant for GM, Chrysler, Ford, and Toyota. Wiegert is one of those exceptional car and vehicle product designers whose creativity was not limited by terms like styling, optimum miles per gallon, or 'cutting production costs,' because he is the total vehicle systems designer and engineer. A supercar should be perfect in every single detail, and perfection takes time and money. To do it yourself without the backing of a large company is not an easy task.

Wiegert's next creation, the prototype of a WX8 hypercar, was shown unfinished – but showing force and direction – in 2007. It was an experiment to judge reaction to a new Vector, and over the next two years, Wiegert spent time advancing and improving the design details of the vehicle. Every square inch of the WX8 was changed; new headlamps and a reworked front make it a fascinating supercar … sorry, hypercar. There is a difference. Its 10-litre V8 engine, based on a Can Am racer and an off-shore racing boat, is capable of producing over 2000bhp, and allows the car to reach speeds in excess of 300mph. Zero to 60mph takes just 2.2 seconds or less – now that's what a hypercar is all about. Aircraft engineering is ever-present in Wiegert's new prototype. As well as certain mechanics derived from aeronautics, the dashboard is designed to resemble the instrument panel of a jet fighter, just like all Vector designs. The WX8 is still in development, but it is only a matter of time before Wiegert's dream car is ready. To bring the latest model to completion, more investors are needed, investors who would share Wiegert's passion for advanced car technology, regardless of the country they are from; in Wiegert's eyes, the world is "a beautiful and blended mix of great nationalities."

Roumen ANTONOV

It is not always the case that everything new is simply something old that has been long-forgotten. But, over the last 50 years, not a single car manufacturer has come up with a radically new development. It sometimes seems that all they can do is improve and hone the technical achievements of Ford, Olds, Royce, and other bright minds of the early 20th century. Other branches of science, such as computing and nanotech, have reached previously unforeseen levels of progress, but unfortunately, the same cannot apparently be said about motoring. As it turns out, though, it is indeed possible to invent something completely new and unprecedented, even in car technology. Most interestingly, the man who tried to make a revolutionary car engine wasn't even born in a country with an automotive heritage – he grew up and studied in communist Bulgaria.

The way the new engine works is very complicated. This is an excerpt from Antonov's own explanation:

"This is an engine with tacking pistons. Its main principle is to provide a four-stroke cycle for one crankshaft revolution. To achieve a change in the volume of its combustion chamber, the Antonov engine uses a system of a deformable parallelogram, which is made of two pistons, both connected to two crankshafts. The combustion chamber is located in the middle of this parallelogram. The two crankshafts are forced to turn in the opposite way by a series of pinions. When the crankshafts revolve, the volume of the combustion chamber decreases twice to a minimum and increases twice to a maximum. When the crankshafts rotate, the chamber trajectory goes through the intake port, the sparkplugs and the exhaust port. At the beginning of the first phase,

the chamber volume is at its minimum, but further to the crankshaft's rotation, the volume expands until the moment when the consecutive sides of the parallelogram make 90° angles. At the same time, the left rod moves, uncovers the intake port and, thanks to the increase in volume, makes the mixture of air and fuel to be sucked up.

"Whilst the crankshafts continue to rotate, the chamber volume starts decreasing, thus changing the angles between the sides of the parallelogram. Once the crankshafts have reached a certain angle, the left rod shuts the intake port. The reduction in the chamber volume then compresses the

A glance inside the unbelievably sophisticated mechanism of the 'four-stroke.' (Courtesy Roumen Antonov)

The 'four-stroke' engine on the testing stand. How much power can we squeeze out of it? (Courtesy Roumen Antonov)

Two Aixam microcars about to race – Antonov's engine versus a conventional one. (Courtesy Roumen Antonov)

locked-up gas. Just before the volume is at its minimum, a spark is generated in the chamber and starts the combustion. The combustion takes place and the pressure reaches its maximum. This pressure is transferred to the crankshafts and generates an engine torque while bringing the parallelogram to its maximum volume. The continuous rotation of the crankshafts creates, in turn, a decrease in the chamber volume. At this stage, the right rod opens the exhaust port which remains open during the whole process. When the chamber reaches its minimum volume, the port is shut by the same rod. The chamber and the parallelogram are now in a position where the whole cycle can start over again."

Called the 'four-stroke' Antonov engine, this remarkable gadget was prepared for the 2002 Paris Motor Show. Shortly before the show, Roumen Antonov finished working on a fully functional prototype and fitted it on the popular Mega Aixam two-seater micro-car, which was the perfect vehicle for this type of engine.

The prototype weighed just 60lb. With maximum revs of 1650, and output of 6.26bhp, the engine produced 26Nm torque. It was very hard to estimate its displacement because the volume of the combustion chamber changes continuously.

You might ask why would somebody invent a new internal combustion engine? Antonov's engine surpasses conventional engines in several different parameters. It doesn't need balancing because the internal vibrations are so insignificant that it is silent enough as it is. The most important benefit of Antonov's engine is a lower mechanical energy loss. This engine fulfils the usual four-stroke cycle on one rotation of a crankshaft, whereas the piston engine takes two rotations to perform four strokes. Less movement means less friction – Antonov's engine is very economical. It also has fewer parts than a piston engine, which makes for a simpler and cheaper manufacturing process.

Antonov's achievements in the field of automotive technology did not stop with a new engine; he also looked at new ways to improve the construction of an automatic gearbox. It is generally known that automatic gearboxes are expensive and sometimes unreliable. There's nothing we can do about it, and not everyone enjoys shifting gears manually – people are getting lazy, and you cannot blame them for this. Probably the

The Rumen prototype – inspired by Bugatti. (Courtesy Roumen Antonov)

The side view of the Rumen. (Courtesy Roumen Antonov)

biggest problems in automatic gearboxes arise on account of the hydraulics. In the late '80s, Antonov began working on a gearbox that wouldn't rely on complicated hydraulics so much. As a matter of fact, Antonov's gearbox is something in between an automatic and a manual one. He isn't the first inventor who has tried to make a manual box with automatic gear shift, but the previous attempts haven't been too successful.

Antonov's gearbox manages without a complicated torque converter, and to achieve six speeds, it needs only two planetary gearsets (a conventional six-speed transmission would need three). There is almost no loss of energy in Antonov's gearbox – it is 30 per cent more efficient than a usual hydraulic automatic gearbox. Besides, it is small in size and comparatively cheap to produce. Whereas the production of a 'normal' automatic gearbox costs anywhere between $1100 to $1500, it is estimated only $675 will be necessary to build Antonov's gearbox.

The interior of the Rumen is full of nostalgia. (Courtesy Roumen Antonov)

Roumen Antonov began to experiment with a four-speed gearbox, but after a while he managed to add two more speeds. He remains confident that it is possible to add more gears, and that the future belongs to multi-speed transmissions, because they are more economical and potentially improve a car's dynamics. Initially, the gearbox would be produced for small front-wheel drive cars with a perpendicular engine layout. Heavy-duty variation would be available, too, but it is the small cars that need a new type of transmission. It is known that small cars and automatic gearboxes hardly ever work together because the latter are too heavy for the former to carry. One of the prototypes Antonov made was just 10in long.

Soon after the new gearbox was announced, General Motors, Honda, Peugeot and some other producers became interested in Antonov's invention. Honda has already acquired a non-exclusive licence to use Antonov's six-speed gearbox (non-exclusive means that Antonov might sell the licence to other companies too). Although Honda was interested in the technology, at the time of writing there is nothing to suggest that the gearbox might be used on a production car. Meanwhile, the one-man-orchestra, Roumen Antonov, has stepped down as chairman of Antonov PLC to pursue scientific research in the field of medicine. The company is now based in Warwickshire, England, and run by Dutch corporate shark Jos Haag. The manufacturing part of operations has gone to China after signing an agreement with a large car manufacturer there; another example of how quickly Europe is losing its industry.

Not only is Antonov a genius engineer, he also has an eye for a car's visual side as well. He was always fascinated with the style of the late 1930s, and for that very reason his first and so far only car, named the '4Stroke,' pays homage to prewar car design. Without doubt, Antonov found his inspiration in the Bugatti Type 57SC Atlantic. He

A view through the rear window – red leather and quality veneer everywhere.
(Courtesy Roumen Antonov)

planned to equip the lightweight car with motorcycle engines – buyers would be able to choose between a smaller 42in³ engine with 54bhp, and the biggest 73in³ engine with as much as 100bhp power. Considering that the 4Stroke weighs only 880lb, you can imagine how dynamic this 3.5-metre runabout would be. According to estimates, the maximum speed of the 4Stroke would be 100 or 112mph, depending on the engine volume.

The body is made of a light composite material, and the interior has a great deal of exclusivity and charm, upholstered in natural red leather, decorated with lacquered wood and heaps of shining knick-knacks. If you're keen on nostalgia, then this car is a must-have. An extra luxury package was designed for people with even higher expectations, including air conditioning and many other modern conveniences. The approximate retail price of this car is unexpectedly low at €30,000.

The rounded back makes this little car very appealing. (Courtesy Roumen Antonov)

Either the car is too small or the driver too tall. This time it is the latter.
(Courtesy Roumen Antonov)

The car soon increased in weight (to 1200lb), and received a proper car engine: a small Peugeot 107 unit. Antonov said he would eventually offer the car with his own four-stroke engine and automatic transmission, but it will need more road testing to make this possible.

Some time ago, there were rumours that the car would go into small-scale production, but after changing the prototype's name to Rumen, the car is still a 'work in progress.' Having first appeared on Mr Antonov's drawing board in 1991, 20 years later it is still his little hobby. However, he never says never – if the automotive industry picks up, he might consider producing the car after all. Besides, his dream was to build a car, not to produce cars, and he has certainly fulfilled that.

Guy NEGRE

Can you imagine what the ideal fuel of the future would be like? It wouldn't produce any hazardous by-products and it would be cheap and safe. Well, this ideal fuel is of natural origin and there are 5000 trillion tonnes of this stuff in the world. It will never run out because the source is renewable. This may sound like audacious science fiction, but it is not: this fuel is in abundance all around us – it is the air we breathe.

So, is it really possible to build a car with an air engine? It is absolutely possible, and not only in theory. Air vehicle prototypes have been built, and very soon they will go on assembly lines to be produced on a mass scale.

The first air engine was built by a Franco-Polish inventor, Louis Mékarski, in around 1890. Construction of an air engine is simple enough, although it must be said, before we rejoice too much, that an air engine which would work without an additional energy source hasn't been invented yet. Otherwise, it would be a perpetuum mobile – although the air engine has high efficiency, it is certainly not that.

Let's examine how it works. Compressed air is carried on board in a safe pressure tank. The compressed air flows into a chamber where it expands and simultaneously cools. That's how thermodynamics work – a gas will cool if pressure drops. Due to expansion, the air drives a piston down. The air is reheated by the ambient temperature (from the sun), and it is forced into the second chamber where it expands again, driving a cylinder up. And so it continues over and over again.

As electric energy is consumed to start the car and compress the air, you might argue that, from an economic perspective, this vehicle is nothing more than an electric car. However, there is a difference. An air engine is more efficient and consumes fewer resources because it uses solar energy, which is free. For the engine to work, it needs ambient heat that comes directly from the sun, even in the winter. It is quite

So that's what an air motor looks like ... (Courtesy MDI Enterprises SA)

MDI OneFlowAir makes another appearance in a car show. (Courtesy MDI Enterprises SA)

difficult to estimate the efficiency of an air engine; however, if you compare it with a conventional four-stroke petrol engine, the latter wastes two-strokes on gas exchange, while an air-engine makes use of every movement that takes place, converting it into mechanical energy.

If air engines are so good, why did nobody introduce them a long time ago? The main obstacle for inventors to overcome was insufficient air compression. Some time ago, you would have needed a high capacity electric motor to compress the air to the required pressure. Using modern technology, it is possible to prepare the necessary quantity of air in a reservoir that would easily fit in a small size car.

Up until 1991, air cars were nothing more than the dreams and visions of enthusiasts. Some experimental models were made, but the idea of producing those cars was utopian indeed. Almost 20 years ago, Guy Negre founded company MDI (Motor Development International). He asserted that he would make an air car that that would gradually go into mass production. The small company, which employed a staff of just 50, set to work, and the first MDI prototype soon appeared. At that time, Negre was considered to be rather eccentric, but then in 2000 he received an order to make taxi cabs for the capital of Mexico, and the critical remarks ceased. Mexico City was regarded as the most polluted city in the world. Its residents were breathing a smog cocktail instead of oxygen. For that very reason, the mayor of Mexico City was ready to approach the problem using very drastic measures. He wanted to clear the fleet of aged green Volkswagen Beetles that were used as taxis, because there were only a few of them that were less than 30 years old. Unfortunately, the deal never came to fruition.

Negre's car is technically rather simple. It is equipped with a two-cylinder air engine, but his car doesn't need a heavy and complicated pump. It carries a reservoir of air compressed to 300bar. The range of an MDI air car is 60 miles, which is enough for urban driving. However, the latest Negre prototypes are dual-fuel vehicles, making them a sort of hybrid. An alternative internal combustion engine is available when the car needs a power boost or when the air runs out.

All MDI car bodies are made of light glass fibre. The range includes four different models, starting from the funky three-seater AirPod, which looks like an embellished phone booth, and ending with the CityFlowAir, which is a proper car, seats 6 people, and looks confident enough on a highway. The middle of the range is made up of two compact urban vehicles, OneFlowAir and MiniFlowAir.

A Mexican taxi driver enjoys a test drive in an early MDI prototype. (Courtesy MDI Enterprises SA)

MDI OneFlowAir roams the streets. (Courtesy MDI Enterprises SA)

OneFlowAir weighs just 380kg (that's dry weight). It is a nice little runner and only 3.6 metres in length. A mono-fuel variation has a 300-litre air tank on board, which will provide enough energy to cover 60 miles. A dual-fuel model will have a smaller air tank, but also an additional internal combustion engine. It is loosely estimated that a dual-fuel OneFlowAir would have a range of 500 miles.

A small commercial vehicle with a half-ton load capacity is available too. All air cars have a small electric device on board called an alternator – it performs the duties of a starter, clutch and brake power regeneration, and acts as a compressor. You can connect the car to a standard 230V electricity source, and the device will top up the air reservoir in four short hours in home conditions. So, if you don't mind the limited range you get when you drive on air only, you will never need to refuel while on the go.

If there were specially adapted filling stations selling compressed air (there are already a few in Germany and France), it would be possible to quick-fill the car in just three minutes. The MDI would have a very low operating cost – topping up would cost around \$2. How much petrol can you buy for two bucks?

What about the price then? The car must cost a fortune to make ... ? In fact, the construction of an MDI is pretty simple, and according to MDI it would be prepared to sell its basic model for as little as €5000. This is very hard to believe, as the price might increase once the car enters the mass-scale production environment and faces all the unknown challenges pertaining to it. But even if the price doubled, there must surely be many people who would be happy to pay €10,000 for a low-maintenance and low-cost green car. Besides, the car really is as simple as it could possibly be. It lacks the majority of parts that our petrol vehicles have, and probably the most expensive part of the air car is its fibreglass body and the air tank.

In the past, the air tank was the biggest safety concern as, allegedly, it could blow up and kill people with the resulting shrapnel. The truth is that there would be no shrapnel in such an event. The air-tank of the MDI is made of a strong, woven carbon fibre, so if it exploded there would be no bits flying through the air. Besides, the pressure in an MDI's air-tank is 300bar – the same as in a scuba-diving cylinder. How often have you heard about a scuba-diver killed by an exploding cylinder? Even if an explosion happened (a freak high-speed crash or similar), air holds much less energy than petrol. If you blow up one litre of compressed air, you get 50Wh energy, whereas if you blow up a litre of petrol, the energy released is almost 190 times higher: 9500Wh.

So why do environmentalists like this car so much? Is it because MDI is a zero emission vehicle? Well, actually it is not zero emission. Electricity is consumed when the air tank is filled, and if this electricity comes from a coal powerplant, an MDI car will contribute to some CO_2 emissions, albeit indirectly. The reason it is so environmentally friendly is that, while driving around the city, it cleans the air. The car is equipped with a carbon block filter that takes all the major pollutants and heavy metals out of the air. So, basically, an MDI is a mobile air filter, and although the volume of clean air emitted by one car is relatively insignificant, several thousand of these cars in a city would certainly make a difference.

As for Guy Negre, he is presently neither a futile dreamer (his work hasn't ended in failure), nor a fully-fledged car producer. His dream of mass-scale production of MDI cars is yet to be realised, but the staying power of this man is truly remarkable. Almost 20 years have passed since he began the development of his unique cars. Although he was confident production would start in the year 2000, it never happened due to lack of investors, minor technical difficulties, and the worldwide political situation.

Negre came one step closer to his dream in 2007, when he secured a deal with India's largest car producer, TATA, which now owns an exclusive licence to produce the air car in India. Although TATA's official line is that the air car is not yet ready to be

MDI AirPod – green by nature, green by colour. (Courtesy MDI Enterprises SA)

driven on the streets, it is very positive about the collaboration with the famous French inventor, and looking forward to putting the air car on an assembly line. This deal also means that Negre has more money to pour into perfecting the construction of the cars; however, he still needs more investors to help him set up his unique industrial concept. Investors, though, are quite reluctant, because as with all new technologies, it may take years for the results and money to be seen.

Negre seems to be a dyed-in-the-wool optimist. He has decided to franchise his industrial concept and offer turnkey factories or micro-plants for people interested in assembling and selling his cars. This concept has many benefits. A person dreaming about making cars can get a foothold in the industry without a multi-million investment. Small factories manufacturing environmentally-friendly goods are a nice way to boost economy and fight unemployment. It is especially appealing for European countries that have recently seen their industry moving to Asia.

Negre currently has a list of people who would be interested in taking on a franchise once the car design is finalised and ready for production. If the Frenchman managed to realise his target production volume (5000 to 10,000 cars a month), he would soon become a very rich person indeed. This course of events would mean a revolution in the car industry. Other inventors would be encouraged to continue research into alternative means of motoring, and the large car producers would no longer hide their new technologies in the labs. However, we have to be patient. Although MDI is closer than ever to actually starting the production of the cars, its model range still has some way to go before it is perfect.

A close-up of an AirPod. (Courtesy MDI Enterprises SA)

AirPod surprises holidaymakers in Nice, France. Notice the way the door opens.
(Courtesy MDI Enterprises SA)

PART TWO

TIMES AND COUNTRIES

PANHARD & LEVASSOR

The company that started car production in France has undeservedly fallen into oblivion. After the Second World War, Panhard & Levassor (or P&L) appeared to have lost its touch, but it still continued to produce its cars until 1967, leaving behind a wealth of experience inherited by Citroën. Panhard & Levassor is not only the oldest car enterprise in France, but also the founder of modern car architecture. Amazingly, the modern layout with the engine in the front and rear-wheel drive was first used on a production car in 1891.

The French car industry began in earnest in 1887. The origins of the industry were in Germany, but it was France that took to the idea of motorisation like a duck to water. French people had shown more interest in horseless carriages than their German neighbours. There were of course sceptics, but far fewer than in Germany.

Being a very good businessman, Gottlieb Daimler – the godfather of the internal combustion engine – knew that it was important to maintain relations with other countries. He chose a Belgian lawyer, Edouard Sarazin, as a representative of his company in France. The two first met back in 1872, when Daimler was still technical director of Deutz AG Gasmotorenfabrik in Cologne. Sarazin was selling Daimler's gas engines to French manufacturers. In 1887, Sarazin began talks with Emile Levassor, one of the owners of P&L, about producing internal combustion engines for the French market. Unfortunately, they didn't finish – Sarazin developed kidney disease and died. The role of powering the French car industry went by default to Sarazin's wife, Louise, who approached both parties – Daimler and Levassor – to let them know that she was ready to continue what her husband had initiated. She went to Kannstadt in 1888 to meet Gottlieb Daimler and prepare the necessary documentation to sell the licence to his engines in French territory. Women in business was a very unusual concept in the 19th century, and would remain so for at least half a century more; still, Gottlieb Daimler was open minded and happily agreed to give Louise a chance. In fact, she was a very shrewd businesswoman. When P&L eventually began producing the engines, she pocketed 8 per cent of all sales. She got the licence from Gottlieb Daimler at a 12 per cent fee, but sold it on to P&L for 20 per cent, keeping the difference.

Panhard & Levassor, then a well-known manufacturer of woodworking machinery, took a great interest in Daimler's invention. In fact, Rene Panhard – the company's other owner – liked to dabble with metal himself. He had created a prototype of an internal combustion engine in 1876, but it was useless due to extremely low revs.

Meanwhile, celebrations of the centenary of the French revolution were in full swing. The culmination of the festivities coincided with the opening of the Paris World Fair of 1889. Many prominent people were invited, and Gottlieb Daimler, with his car, was amongst them. However, he was a little late for the fair and couldn't get a separate exhibition stand for display, so got permission to exhibit his car beside the saw-frames of Panhard & Levassor. The French public welcomed new invention, and local businessmen hurried to enquire about Daimler's engine patent. But it was already safe in the hands of a certain lady, who knew exactly what to do with it.

Emile Levassor was not only a talented engineer, but also a rather charming person. In 1890, Madame Sarazin became his wife, and together they began working towards the motorisation of France. Many people said in those days that it was a marriage of convenience, especially because the puritanical society of the 19th century considered that a widow's duty was to mourn her deceased husband for the rest of her life. People who knew them better said that the two were driven by the same passion.

Levassor set about constructing his first car, and in 1890 it was almost finished. The frame was mostly made of wood, and the V2 engine was placed in the middle of the car under the floor. The four-seater car had two rows of seats with the passenger row facing in the opposite direction. It was quite awkward, and P&L started looking at other layout options. The next model had the two-cylinder engine in the front and the drive transferred to the rear wheels. This new configuration made the assembling easier, gave the driver much better control, and made the car more pleasurable to drive.

The capacity of the engine made according to Daimler's licence was 1.2 litres, and it produced a 'staggering' 2.5bhp – so you can see how far car engines have come in just a hundred years. Still, the car could go at 18mph, which was pretty fast for an engine so weak. P&L was officially the first company that started to produce cars for sale. Although Karl Benz and Gottlieb Daimler and some other engineers had created prototypes of a horseless carriage before P&L, it was the twosome that triggered production for the French motoring industry. Ironically, Daimler did not sell his first car until 1892.

Soon, Emile Levassor took an interest in motor racing, as he believed that it would be a good way to create publicity and stir people's interest. He raced his own cars, and in 1895 he took part in the Paris-Bordeaux-Paris Trail. That was a real feat, as the 730-mile-long trail would take a couple of days to cover, which is why replacement drivers were positioned along the route. Alas, Levassor's replacement driver had overslept at the changeover, and the engineer had to complete the race on his own. Having spent more than 48 hours awake behind the wheel, Levassor won the trophy, leaving the closest follower a good six hours behind.

In 1896, he took part in the Paris-Marseilles-Paris rally and was seriously injured. Unfortunately he never recovered from his injuries, and died the following year, leaving Madame Sarazin-Levassor twice widowed. After his colleague's death, Rene Panhard lost any interest in cars and gave the reins to Arthur Krebs, who eventually succeeded in turning P&L into one of the biggest car manufacturers of the early 20th century.

In 1916, Krebs was replaced as the general manager by Paul Panhard, a distant relative of the company's founder. He gave the company a reputation as an innovator in car fashion. The Dynamic of 1936 is considered to be the most successful and extraordinary model from P&L. When the car was unveiled, many thought it was only a prototype, but it actually hit the production lines in 1937. Some regard it as the most beautiful Art Deco object ever put on wheels. Although the peak of Art Deco's popularity in Europe had passed, the style was still a very strong favourite.

Until the Second World War, the Dynamic remained the only model produced by P&L. The first prototypes featured a driver seat and controls placed in the centre. The power unit was a six-cylinder engine without valves – a sleeve valve engine. These were popular in the high-end prewar cars. Sleeve valve engines were more efficient with a more optimal gas exchange, but they were quite unreliable and oil-consuming. Those engines were almost noiseless, but extremely expensive. It goes without saying that only rich people could afford a P&L car.

A 1899 Panhard & Levassor 8CV – the start of a legend.
(Courtesy Gilles Blanchet)

Panhard Dynamic – a symphony of Art Deco on wheels. (Courtesy David Saunders)

After the war, P&L managers hoped to resume production of luxury cars, but the French government had other plans, and introduced a crisis economy. Only cheap car producers could receive raw material and other resources. Suddenly, Renault found itself in a privileged position. Not long ago it had been a private company, but then it was nationalised, and the government began pumping huge sums of money into the enterprise, leaving other car producers in a rather disadvantaged position. Nobody at P&L understood anything about small cars; they were accustomed to creative work and using their imagination.

In spite of the circumstances, P&L decided to give it a go and play by the new rules. A lightweight compact model, the Dyna, appeared in 1946. It was quirky and unusual, but people quite liked it, though mainly for its low fuel consumption. The company had reverted from a posh V6 powerhouse to a two-cylinder engine – just like when it had started in 1889. The Dyna had a two-cylinder, air-cooled, boxer-type engine, with a capacity of 610cc. It produced only 24bhp, but, due to the car's low weight, it could go at speeds of up to 70mph. Its aluminium body weighed only 560kg.

Though P&L did its very best to experiment with extraordinary shapes and technology, the new France didn't understand its 'haute' design. Amidst great financial difficulties, P&L's designers kept working on a brand new model called the 24 CT, which was destined to be the last car it ever made. Although the car did well in rallies, its success didn't translate into sales, mainly because P&L lacked good dealer coverage. At that time, its cars were represented by Citroën dealers. Matters didn't improve, and the company was absorbed by Citroën in 1965. The last car to bear a Panhard badge was produced in 1967.

40 years later, the badge has been reborn. In 2005, Auverland – a small French company specialising in light military vehicles – bought the rights to use the name Panhard, and now all its brand-new 4x4s are called that. This was a move to re-establish Auverland's public image. Will it work? We shall see. Auverland is a national treasure in France because it is the only company that produces a real French SUV. Commercially, it has had moderate success, but is yet to establish itself abroad. However, the cars produced by the company are sturdy and make good workhorses, so one day we might well see the return of Panhard.

The Panhard Dynamic was a huge and impressive car. (Public domain image)

Opposite: A page from a Panhard 24 sales brochure. (Courtesy Phil Seed)

Panhard Dyna – both the actual car and the advert show influences of the Art Deco movement, even though it is 1957. (Courtesy Phil Seed)

THE LAST ROMANTICS

Looking back over automotive history, it seems that France has never felt the need for big and expensive cars. The traditions of motorisation of various nations are as different as their cultures and cuisine. Even though many French people are wealthy and have refined taste, you will rarely see big and expensive automobiles in French cities. A car in France is not a status symbol. It is more important that it doesn't use much fuel and is easy to park. It is rather strange that this romantic nation is so practical when it comes to cars. French car manufacturers rarely produced huge, luxurious cars after the Second World War, and even if somebody had tried it, it would be almost guaranteed to be a disaster.

This is what happened to the genius Louis Renault when he unveiled one of the most admirable cars of all times – the 1922 Renault 40CV, and the 1929 Reinastella that followed it. These were both huge and expensive cars that received many caustic or even bitter remarks from the public, although many aristocrats dreamt secretly of owning the beautiful Renault. While in the same period of time, Rolls-Royce, across the English Channel, easily sold thousands of luxury cars, Renault only managed to hit the low hundreds. History repeats itself, of course – the Renault Safrane of 1992, which was considered an excellent car in many aspects, didn't meet with the success it deserved because it was anything but economic. The Safrane was loved by the English, Italians, and Germans, but was totally underestimated on its home ground. Today there is the big Citroën C6, which, again, never really received its due acclaim.

Fortunately, there are always the Frenchmen who are not bothered about the practical aspects of a car. They believe that a car should be big and showy, and a dream-come-true – not just a vehicle that beats the competiton for a shorter body or a lower fuel consumption. The Voisin, Delage, Delahaye, Hotchkiss, Talbot, Facel Vega, and Monica were all beautiful cars, and they took the idea of motoring as far from mass production as possible. They were masterpieces; and many of them duly appreciated only after the death of their creators.

After the war, the gap in the market was there for such a car – but who was courageous enough to try and fill it? There was someone who was interested: Jean Daninos. His metalworking company FACEL (Forges et Ateliers de Construction d'Eure et de Loire) was founded in 1938, and was one of the rare wartime enterprises that managed to get through the gloomy years and even make a great deal of money on account of the war effort. FACEL manufactured gas generators, aircraft engines and steel sheets. After the war, Daninos continued producing aircraft assemblies, and branched out into other fields too, such as furniture and car bodies.

The first client of FACEL's new design workshop was Panhard, then came Delahaye and Simca. At that time, it would be difficult to call Daninos' work creative – he just produced metalwork according to other designers' sketches. The chance to parade his own visual developments opened up for him when Ford established its French subsidiary. FACEL received an order to make a brand new sports coupé. The

Maestro Jean Daninos working on a sketch.
(Courtesy Amicale Facel Vega, facel-vega.asso.fr)

Ford Comete was born – a rather beautiful car whose fate was decided by the awful quality of the V8 engine supplied by Ford. However, the idea of a powerful sports coupé fascinated Daninos and he decided to risk his financial security, despite the unfavourable situation in the luxury car market.

Together with fellow engineer Jacques Brasseur, he created a prototype named 'Vega,' in honour of a star. This classic and tasteful car, the Facel Vega FVS, was unveiled at the 1954 Paris Motor Show and it was clear that the public loved it. In contrast to the fashion at that time, the car had no chromium plating and the glittery effect of certain parts was achieved with polished steel.

It would be extremely difficult to build an original engine, so Jean Daninos visited Detroit and picked the best of what was available – a V8 of Chrysler De Soto Firedome. It was just the ticket for the new French supercar – powerful and reliable. He also took a Chrysler Torqueflite automatic transmission to go with the engine. The gear shifting was very convenient – the driver could operate it with the help of buttons. The Torqueflite is still one of the best gearboxes ever, even after 50 years. Serious car enthusiasts preferring manual gearboxes could opt for a local Pont-à-Mousson transmission. Driving a manual Facel Vega was a real adventure. The clutch was so heavy that only the strongest men could handle it properly. Despite all this, many people seemed to be attracted to the idea of a manual Vega, as it handled like a real sports car.

The FVS was produced until 1959, when it was replaced by the HK500 – the best car Facel Vega has ever produced. It was irresistibly elegant and equipped with a bigger 6.3-litre Chrysler engine. The 180bhp engine had enviable specs: zero to sixty took just nine seconds and the top speed was 130mph. It would take powerful brakes to bring the beast to a halt. That, however, wasn't Daninos' plan – he had equipped the car with weak hydraulic brakes not fit for its weight and speed. In the '50s, Europe didn't really have any set standards for automobile brakes, and this small area of neglect didn't cost the car its reputation. Only one serious accident involving a Facel Vega was recorded: the famous French writer and philosopher Albert Camus was killed when his publisher and friend, Michel Gallimard, lost control of a Facel Vega.

In the first two years after the Paris show, Jean Daninos built 46 cars. It was a promising result for a new company that didn't have any prewar car manufacturing traditions or authority. The price was another factor – a Vega cost around $7000, which was much cheaper than a Rolls-Royce or another imported luxury car.

Daninos wanted to create something new and beautiful. He revised the car's design and replaced the Firedome with a newer and more powerful 5.5-litre Chrysler V8. In 1956, a full-size four-door limo, the Facel Vega Excellence, made its debut at the Paris Motor show. It had taken another two years to prepare, but the result was stunning – it was one of the most beautiful cars of the '50s, and allegedly the fastest European limo of that period. The car could do 125mph, a speed unsurpassed until 1963 by the Maserati Quattroporte, which had a top speed of 143mph. The Facel Vega Excellence was a very beautiful car, and, for that reason owners often forgave all of its imperfections. One of the biggest and most amusing defects was to do with the car's back doors. It had a pillarless construction and featured so-called 'suicide doors' which opened in opposite directions, allowing more convenient access into and out of the car.

As there was no pillar, the body of the Excellence wasn't rigid enough, and it skewed a little each time the car did a fast turn, which caused the door to unlock and burst open. Imagine the shock it gave the passengers! The owners had to use a little of their ingenuity to figure out how to keep the doors shut. Some simply used a bit of rope to tie the doors together. Despite its technical oddities, the car cost $12,800, placing

Stirling Moss (later Sir) and his wife with their amazing Facel Vega HK500 on George V Avenue in Paris. (Courtesy Amicale Facel Vega)

Facel Vega Excellence caught on camera in the Netherlands.
(Courtesy Eduard Hattuma)

Studebaker had an idea to Americanise the Facel Vega Excellence. Notice the classic Studebaker grille. (Courtesy Alden Jewell)

it at the very top of the ladder with Rolls-Royce and Mercedes. Daninos managed to produce only 152 units of the Excellence, yet it had a much bigger potential. Even dubious critics couldn't kill the reputation of the car. Many famous people chose to drive it, including, for example, actress Ava Gardner, the prince of Saudi Arabia, the king of Morocco and the president of Mexico. They wanted to persuade the president of France, Charles de Gaulle, into buying 'locally,' but he refused the Excellence because he was a patriot from head to toe, and allegedly couldn't cope with the fact that it was not a 100 per cent French car; it had an American engine under the bonnet.

Facel Vega always won the admiration of the rich and famous. An HK500 has been seen in the garages of 'Josephine' Tony Curtis, singer Dean Martin, racing drivers Sir Stirling Moss, Rob Walker, and Maurice Trintignant, artist Pablo Picasso, the Shah of Persia, ex-Beatle Ringo Starr, and the aforementioned Ava Gardner, who actually owned three Vegas.

In 1959, Jean Daninos decided to open the brand to a larger section of the public by making the cars more accessible. That was probably his mistake. He considered

Facellia was destined to compete with Porsche.
(Courtesy Alexander Z, released under Creative Commons licence)

it the right time to capture the mass market. It would have been a good idea to offer people an elegant and sporty coupé at a reasonable price, if Daninos had only been a little more careful. He constructed a four-seater coupé called the Facellia, and possibly being influenced by the ardent patriotism of Charles de Gaulle, decided to equip it with a dubious 'made in France' engine. The evil mastermind behind the fiasco of the Facel Vega was Pont-à-Mousson – the company that made the transmissions for Daninos.

The Pont-à-Mousson 1.6-litre engine was a total disaster. They calculated it to have 140bhp power, but when the engine was finished and tested, it could only output 114bhp. It was a huge risk mounting an untested engine on a mass production car. Furthermore, Daninos had intended to assemble the engines in his own factory from parts provided by Pont-à-Mousson. He did not account for the fact that his mechanics lacked experience working with engines – up until this point they had received assembled sealed engines from Detroit, and all they had to do was fix the engine to the frame and join it to the gearbox and other parts.

Daninos' plan was to compete with the Porsche 90, Alfa Romeo Giulietta and other sports cars by producing 500 units of the Facellia each year. The new car was revealed later in 1959. People loved it – it was a very pleasant car, and, aimed at young middle-class Frenchmen, it really promised to be a hit. Unfortunately, when the car came on the market its faults became obvious. There was not much 'go' in the Pont-à-Mousson engines, and the dealer centres were inundated with complaints. The car that had now been put into mass production started leaking some serious money.

Daninos hurried to change the engine to a modern Volvo P1800 power unit, and renamed the car the 'Facel Vega III,' but the Facellia's image had already been irreversibly damaged. The debut of a luxury coupé, the Facel Vega II, couldn't save the day. The slender coupé went from 0 to 60 in seven seconds and could maintain a top speed of 140mph. It followed the winning formula – American engine plus French

Jean Daninos taking a trip down memory lane. (Courtesy Gilles Blanchet)

elegance – but, after the big flop of the Facellia, it seemed that the rich in France didn't want to hear about the Vega any more. In 1963, Daninos lost control of his company as it went into administration. He still managed to develop a new car, the Facel Vega 6, before the business was closed in 1964. It had produced around 3000 cars in total.

Jean Daninos reached a great age, dying in 2001 aged 95. Nowadays, a well-preserved Vega is highly sought-after and relatively as expensive as it was in the '50s. The most expensive models in the aftermarket are the Excellence and, however ironic it may seem now, a Facellia with an original Pont-à-Mousson engine.

Although Facel Vega set a new standard of elegance in the European car industry, Jean Daninos achieved something that he possibly never realised: he set a precedent of pairing a small European car maker with a big American engine. This would prove to be a very successful formula in the coming decades, and in fact it still is a winning formula for some privately-owned motor works. Iso Rivolta, De Tomaso, Jensen, and many others followed his example, proving that multimillion investments were not necessary to start producing cars. Car production really had become more accessible, and people who dreamt about immortalising their name on a car badge could finally do so.

The early '60s saw many budding car entrepreneurs following the example of Jean Daninos, and a real boom of car works were opened up in Europe. Currently, there are hundreds of companies making original cars in small series. The majority of them use ready-made engines from Detroit. Unfortunately, there are still very few small carmakers in France.

After the sad bankruptcy of Facel Vega, absolute stillness prevailed over the French supercar market for a couple of years. Nobody wanted to repeat the failure of previous dreamers. However, France wouldn't be France if convenient stagnation hadn't been disturbed by a daredevil.

Historically, watchmakers, bicycle producers and aircraft engineers have often successfully ventured into car production, and in 1967, a railwayman joined this mixed company. Jean Tastevin, a rich industrialist from the picturesque Loire district, decided he would be the right person to become the next car maverick, and liven up France's ailing exotic car market. Tastevin managed CFPM – a huge steel works that also produced rail coaches in Balbigny. Being a talented businessman and an art connoisseur blessed with outstanding taste, Jean didn't really contemplate all the idiosyncrasies of car engineering, and acted too hastily with too wide a scope. The fuel crisis and speed limits that came into effect across Europe at the time eventually turned Jean's dreams into futile fantasies.

Tastevin wasn't a complete novice when it came to cars, however. He had acquired an impressive antique car collection, and was famous for restoring some of the cars himself. His passion was British cars and the Italian Maserati, and Jean wanted to combine all that he thought was good and beautiful in one car. He had some ideas, and approached British racing car designer Christopher J Lawrence with a query regarding tuned engines. Their correspondence and later acquaintanceship resulted in Lawrence being involved in the whole process of building the car from scratch.

It was 1968 when Lawrence set to work. Several chassis and the first full-bodied prototype were built at the LawrenceTune workshop, and Jean named the car Monica, in honour of his wife, who later took an active part in the decision-making. However, the Tastevins weren't particularly happy with the first two prototypes. Lawrence had managed to come up with a very lightweight design, which would suit the small Martin V8 engine intended for the car. Many thought that Lawrence's prototype was very beautiful, but Tastevin eventually commissioned Tony Rascanu – a little known Romanian designer – to improve the visual image. This was how the car got its pop-up

The very first of the Monica prototypes, as it was in 2010. The original colour was aubergine, and in fact, the car's shape is reminiscent of an aubergine. (Courtesy Brian Chant, Dorset Vintage & Classic Auctions, dvca.co.uk)

Monica 1 from the rear. The car has seen better days, but once restored to its former glory it will be a show stopper. (Courtesy Brian Chant, Dorset Vintage & Classic Auctions)

headlamps and much lower bonnet line. Even Rascanu's design was not deemed good enough, and English designer David Coward had to add the final touch.

At last Jean was satisfied with the result. He had ended up with a car that looked like a mish-mash of Maserati, Ferrari and Aston Martin. Still, it was very unusual, as it was not a coupé but a four-door saloon. Nevertheless, it certainly looked harmonious. Henri Chapron made the wooden forms for production and they were sent to Vignale coachbuilders in Torino, Italy, so that they could build the final prototype for the exhibition.

Now the Monica had turned into a real international project – but wouldn't it be easier and cheaper to build the car entirely in France? Even with the mammoth work accomplished, and the frayed nerves, once again luck wasn't on Jean's side. The owner of Vignale, Alfredo Vignale, died in 1969, and the management of the company changed. The exhibition prototype remained unfinished.

There was nothing for Jean Tastevin to do but to look for another workshop that would finish the prototype, so that the Monica could make its long awaited public debut. He chose an enterprise from across the Channel – Airflow Streamlines. Meanwhile, the news about a new French supercar had reached the press and the rumour spread across France like an avalanche. It was a matter of prestige that France would make luxury cars again, and people were really excited about it. They had a long wait on their hands – preparing the car's mechanical parts proved as big a struggle as designing it.

Disregarding Daninos' positive experience with Chrysler engines, Tastevin apparently thought that it was wrong to produce cars with pre-fab engines. Today, we do not see anything wrong with this method and

Jean Tastevin (right) with his employees. (Courtesy Nathalie Tastevin)

Madame Tastevin was the inspiration behind the Monica project.
(Courtesy Nathalie Tastevin)

The back of the Monica – very '70s and very stylish. (Courtesy Vintage European Automobiles, Canada, vea.qc.ca)

the advantages are obvious – lower production costs, higher reliability, and more convenient repairs – but in the '60s, people thought otherwise. The use of a foreign engine was usually regarded as bad taste. It suggested that the producer wasn't able to make a good enough engine himself.

Tastevin stuck to the original engine with the guru of English motorsport, Ted Martin, who was famous for his Formula 1 engines. What Martin did was to take a full-bodied Formula 1 engine and make it a little bit more civilised. Although Martin's V8 was a good little engine, it was still an F1 engine – a completely different philosophy and approach. It produced 250bhp, but it wasn't enough for Tastevin. The first complete car with Martin's engine weighed only 1070kg – a great achievement for a four-door saloon, but Tastevin didn't think much of it, and continued adding more and more to the weight of the car (air conditioning, electric windows, a wide range of different luxury items and gadgets), until it turned out that Martin's engine was indeed too small for the car.

Tastevin made ambitious plans. The Balbigny motor plant intended to produce at least 400 Monica units a year – a huge amount for a new and inexperienced luxury car brand. Tastevin was soon brought back to reality by the engine mishap. Having recognised, at last, that an original engine on his car was a no-go, Tastevin sent Chris Lawrence to negotiate a deal with Detroit. As neither Ford nor Chevrolet wanted to bother with another 'obscure' European carmaker, the only choice (and the best one, it could be said) was to go for a similar engine to that used in Facel Vegas some years ago – the Chrysler V8. It still resembled the old Chrysler V8 of the '50s; it was still loud and gas-guzzling, but on the other hand, it was powerful, relatively cheap, very reliable, and practically impossible to kill. Now the car weighed almost two tons, and Tastevin realised that it was too much. In the end, the final prototype weighed 1850kg, and could reach a maximum speed of 149mph.

The car was presented at the 1972 Paris motor show, and its debut was coupled with the splendid opening of the motor show. They all loved France's new supercar, but public interest was somewhat diminished when they found out that it was not possible to order the car. A production line wasn't ready at CFPM, and not all the technical problems had been solved. Besides, the car went to the show with Martin's engine because the prototype with a Chrysler powerplant wasn't ready at the time.

A year later, Tastevin repeated the debut of the Monica. Now, at last, it was ready. The car was perfect – in fact, it was too perfect for it to ever be profitable. France's own supercar was ready to make its way to potential buyers, but unfortunately, its second debut coincided with a fuel crisis, which killed off any chance of success for the Monica. Moreover, the government introduced a lower speed limit. A car doing 149mph and only 15mpg no longer made any sense in good old France. It had a price tag of £14,000, which was really too much. You could get a Rolls-Royce Silver Shadow with a long wheel base for £7960, or the huge Phantom VI for £13,100. The Monica's main competitor, the Maserati Quattroporte, cost only £8400, but the real supercar, the Maserati Ghibli, cost £10,200. Another luxury four-seater Lamborghini Espada cost £10,300. All this meant that the Monica was the most expensive production car in the world. So a potential buyer might have asked himself: "Why should I pay through the nose and buy a Monica?"

Many different styles combined into one rather harmonious and elegant car.
(Courtesy Nathalie Tastevin)

Looking at Monica's front, you can hardly tell it is a full-size sedan.
(Courtesy Vintage European Automobiles, Canada)

It would be hard to give an answer. The Monica was a brilliant car; it just had the wrong timing and the wrong price tag. The question is reasonable to a certain extent as, looking at it from a technical point of view, the Monica wasn't any better than a Rolls-Royce or a Ferrari. Of course, the sophisticated de Dion suspension that led to more comfortable driving and all four disc brakes made Monica a worthy car. On the other hand, the choice of engine wasn't the best in the world. People looked quite askance at an original European car that had an American engine under its bonnet. The Iso Rivolta was a similar combination of Italian design and American power, but it was much, much cheaper than Monica. The aura of exclusivity was not enough to keep the venture afloat.

Five years and a staggering 21 prototypes and pre-production vehicles later, the car was ready to be prepared for production. Although Chris Lawrence and his team had planned the production lines, the job of planning the details of the assembly process was given to one Poussot. Instead of preparing the factory for production, he set to secretly de-anglicise the car. After a whole year of tinkering, Jean Tastevin discovered, to his sheer horror, that no progress had been made, and the final result was worse than Lawrence's pre-production version. Chris Lawrence was called in to save the situation again, but, alas, it was too late.

In February 1975, Jean Tastevin finished the production of Monica with only an estimated 8 cars sold. Shortly afterwards, Bob Jankel, the owner of Panther Cars offered to restart the production of Monica. He had followed Tastevin's progress and was of the opinion that Monica was a unique car. He was sure that the car would do better in Britain; however, nothing came of it.

The creator of the Monica was an idealist. Jean Tastevin knew exactly what annoyed him about mass-production cars. Making his own car was an attempt to get rid of all those inconvenient and cheap trifles, which made the everyday life of a motorist almost unbearable. He thought that the most important thing was ergonomics – the driver and passengers should derive pleasure from driving. Can you imagine anything more inconvenient than the design of the door handle? From the opposite side, you cannot really reach it. Tastevin had the idea of making a mechanism that would release the door with a touch of a button. One soft click and the door is open. It also wasn't possible to find the smallest bit of synthetics in Monica's interior. The seats were made of exclusive Connolly leather, and the leather theme continued in the upholstery and the front panel. There were velvet insets and details in valuable wood. The plenitude of leather and velvet stood out perfectly against the beautiful veneer.

Jean didn't intend to reconcile himself to the traditional idea that a sports car should be uncomfortable and manly. All four of the Monica's seats were shaped so that everyone would forget the fact they were driving a sports car; well, at least up to the moment when the speedometer clocked 140mph. Although the car was almost five metres long, its endless bonnet left limited space for the interior. But it was possible to install four comfortable seats in a relatively compact space, mostly thanks to the width of the car. It was a whole 182cm from one side to the other, which was only 4cm less than a Rolls-Royce Silver Shadow.

Only eight commercial models were apparently sold. However, some of the prototypes still exist, mainly residing in private collections or museums. There is no official fan club for Monica cars, and the collectors who own the car are not too keen to exhibit it. On those rare occasions when a Monica appears on an antique car show, it is an instant hit with visitors and enthusiasts. There are a couple of cars in the UK, one in Sweden, the Netherlands, and even the USA. The real fate of all the prototypes is not known.

Jean Tastevin was never content with the Monica's appearance. He made constant changes, but he still wasn't happy. Although this approach is typical of many artists, unfortunately it is not the best approach for car manufacturing. Other car producers put the main accent on perfecting the drawings, then making one or two prototypes, touching it up, and putting it on the production line. In some cases, when money is not an issue, and people have plenty of ambition, the number of prototypes might reach three or four. Jean Tastevin could have probably entered the Guinness Book of records with his 21 prototypes and pre-production versions.

Tastevin was a multi-millionaire and never watched the pennies; however, he spent a good part of his fortune on the car. According to Christopher Lawrence, he spent £1.75 million on the Monica project. People who knew Tastevin well asserted that the fiasco of the Monica didn't break this enterprising Frenchman. He referred to his 8-year span as an automotive entrepreneur a mere business risk. "We all take risks every day without even noticing it," he said.

The man had a vision, but he didn't have a plan of execution. Who knows if the Monica's fate would have been any different if Tastevin had reconciled himself to fewer prototypes, decreased the number of different people involved, and put the car into production before 1969. He would almost certainly have sold more cars, but I don't think the outcome would have changed had he done anything differently. After all, it was the fuel crisis and speed limit that killed off the near-perfect Monica.

***

There have been several other attempts to produce a luxury car in France. Venturi, established in 1984, produced pure French sports cars until 2000, and it struggled to survive all the way through its existence. Nowadays, it is owned by Gildo Pallanca Pastor, a millionaire from Monaco. He is planning to produce a range of electric cars, and is a creator of the first electric sports car, the Venturi Fetish, which appeared at the Paris car show in 2004, before the Tesla Roadster.

The experiments of Renault to create an easily available supercar did not receive the anticipated response. The Alpine of 1985 and the Spider of 1995 were good cars, but the market wasn't there for them. The last mass-produced French luxury car, the Citroën SM, went to rack and ruin in 1975, the same year as the Monica.

This red beauty, the Citroën SM, was one of the last French luxury sportscars. (Copyright: Citroën Communication / Renauld Leblan)

A totally unique car – a presidential cabrio SM Présidentielle created by stretching a standard SM. (Copyright: Citroën Communication)

The saga of the SM began in 1968, just like the project of Jean Tastevin. Citroën had just acquired the famous Italian carmaker Maserati. It wasn't quite sure what to do with the new purchase, and decided to use Maserati's potential and experience to make a new luxury sports car. The Citroën SM (abbreviation of Sport Maserati) was finished in 1970, and remains one of the most extraordinary Citroëns of all time. Although the company was popular during the '50s and '60s with its models that resembled UFOs, nobody believed Citroën would be capable of making a sports car. It was anticipated that this elegant car would compete with Porsche, Jaguar and other gran tourismo models, but it never happened. Citroën managed to sell 13,000 units of the SM before the model was discontinued. Not bad for five years, but one should consider that the majority of SMs went to the USA. It was never popular in France.

Despite this, Citroën proved to the doubtful that sports cars and front-wheel drive are not a utopian combination, but a clever way to build manoeuvrable and comparatively inexpensive cars. Equipped with a 3-litre engine that produced 180bhp, the Citroën SM could reach a speed of 142mph. This car introduced many technical innovations: headlamps that turned with the steering to light the turn, a windscreen wiper that regulated itself automatically depending on the intensity of precipitation, power-assisted steering, and self-regulating headlamps with six elements. However, you will find only four elements on American exports, because six was considered unsafe in the USA.

The Citroën SM was an underestimated car of the future, though unfortunately, it consumed too much fuel to get it anywhere past 1975.

THE END OF THE ROYAL FLEET

In the middle of the 19th century, strange roaring carriages appeared on the roads of Europe. Horse owners were very worried – the puffing devils (named after Londoner Richard Trevithick's steam carriage) frightened the horses, and the poor animals lost their ability to work. Seeing the total disorder on the roads, the British government introduced a rather ridiculous law in 1865 named the Locomotive Act, later nicknamed the 'Red Flag Act.' It limited the maximum speed of self-propelled carriages to 2mph in cities, and 4mph on highways. It also required that each steam carriage should be preceded by a man carrying a red flag, warning coachmen about the terrible danger approaching. As the red-flag men usually walked steadily and vigorously in front of the puffing devil, they were soon nicknamed 'stalkers.' This has nothing to do with the modern meaning of the word.

Around the mid-1890s, as the first cars were imported from the continent, people soon realised the ludicrousness of the Red Flag Act. In fact, the red flag had been abolished in 1878, but the name remained because a stalker still had to walk in front of a moving vehicle. One Harry J Lawson, a bicycle manufacturer from Coventry, used his flair of string-pulling in 1895 to lobby for changes in the law. He wasn't just a motoring enthusiast; he was also involved in the Daimler Motor Company with Frederick Simms, and his dream was to monopolise the British car industry. As a result, the government gave in and repealed the Red Flag Act completely, even increasing the speed limit to 14mph.

Amongst the people, the new legislation began to be known as the Emancipation Act. To celebrate his victory, Lawson organized the Emancipation Run from London to Brighton on 14 November 1896. 33 cars set off from London, and more than half – 17 – managed to arrive in Brighton. This day is officially known as the day of the birth of British motoring. In 1927, the tradition of doing the Emancipation Run resumed and it has been alive ever since, with the exception of some really bad years when it was impossible to complete. Today, it is the oldest motoring event in the world.

Neither Lawson nor Simms made the first ever British motor car. Most likely it was Walter Arnold, who, in 1894, brought a Karl Benz engine over from Germany and built a car. However, there will probably never be consensus on the issue. Some records show that it was Santler, but others say that it was Frederick William Lanchester. It is known for certain that Lanchester built his prototype in 1895, and Santler's and Arnold's attempts were also more of a prototype than a production car. The first commercially produced model, however, is attributed to Harry J Lawson and the Daimler Motor Company, which began producing cars in small series in 1897. He was pretty well off selling bicycles (some still regard Lawson as the father of the modern chain-driven bicycle), but of course Lawson had to convince investors to put up the money for his risky new enterprise.

Coventry was the most obvious choice for the base of the new industry. Out of its 70,000 inhabitants, 40,000 were involved in precision manufacturing – ranging from clocks to bicycles and scientific instruments. An empty cotton mill was chosen to house the motor works. By that time, Lawson had acquired a diverse portfolio of continental patents and licences. He had also established at least seven companies under different names to gain acclaim and importance. Soon, the motor plant began producing cars under licences of Daimler and Bollee. At the turn of the century the legality of some of his patents began to be questioned, and his motoring domination ended in a courtroom. All of the fake companies collapsed one by one. Although some call Harry J Lawson a scam artist, his contribution towards the development of the British car industry is indisputable.

While Lawson kept himself busy attempting to monopolise British motoring, Frederick William Lanchester kept himself out of the business limelight. He confined himself to his barn and tinkered with an engine. He had never seen the engines of Daimler or Benz, but was familiar with the idea, so decided to go his own way.

Lanchester's first engine was so weak that it could barely move the carriage it was mounted on. In 1896 he completed the second prototype, and now the 2-cylinder engine was fully functional. As odd as it sounds today, it had just one valve per cylinder; however, Lanchester's disc valve managed the gas exchange just fine. The next couple of years was spent improving the construction, and in 1898 Lanchester received the Golden Medal at the Automobile Exhibition. The following year, Frederick William Lanchester and his two brothers, George and Frank, formed the Lanchester Engine Company. Sadly, financial success evaded them. Frederick Lanchester had a brilliant mind, and we continue using many of his inventions without knowing that he was the founder of the first truly British car factory.

Lanchester Landaulet of 1913. The company made great cars, but didn't achieve much commercial success. (Courtesy Gilles Blanchet)

THE END OF THE ROYAL FLEET

No other country has had so many car producers as Great Britain. In the very late 1890s, only six or seven people produced cars; by the turn of the century, the number of motor plants and workshops amounted to 90, and by the First World War, 201 enterprises were registered as engine or car body manufacturers – a staggering number for such an early stage in motoring history. Miraculously, the war didn't have a big impact on the British car industry. Local production was also encouraged by imposing rigorous taxes on imported cars. The whole range of American car dealers and the few continental dealers had to leave the country because business was so meagre, with a 33.3 per cent customs duty making foreign cars completely undesirable for English buyers. After the war, the policy on customs duty remained just as rigid. At one time, there was also a tax similar to modern excise duty – each imported car was taxed £1 for every bhp of power. So, a Ford T that would cost a little over £100 now had £24 on top, just because it wasn't made in Britain. The British car industry needed a helping hand from time to time, and it was good to see that the government understood that.

Feeling that the government was taking good care of the industry, British engineers threw themselves into the car business one after another. They adjusted their bicycle and horse carriage workshops to accommodate car assembly, and by 1922 the number of motor plants in Britain had reached its peak – 206 enterprises. Amazingly, 130 of them were located near Coventry. How meagre Detroit looked, compared to this magnificent abundance!

As the demand for luxury cars decreased, and the market became more saturated, many businessmen gradually switched back to making bicycles. Up until the 1960s, the number of British car makers balanced out at around 60, then began to increase on account of kit cars, replica car makers, and privately owned luxury car works. Nowadays, the statisticians have lost count. No-one exactly knows how many car works there are in Britain. Some keep popping up while others go bankrupt to regroup and bounce back again. Some of them are foreign makers who have found that Britain's friendly car registration process makes life much easier. Although there are certain tests to be passed and standards to be met, the Driver and Vehicle Licensing Agency (which approves new models and kit cars) has indirectly stimulated the movement of 'home brew' car manufacturing. Britons haven't lost their motoring roots, and the huge number of amateur races and local car shows is proof of that.

It is a pity that amongst the now functioning car makers, there are no truly British large-scale producers left. Apparently, Morgan Motors and Bristol Cars are the last two heroes standing whose efforts could be remotely regarded as 'large scale.' Morgan – still owned by the founding family – manages to produce 600 cars a year, while Bristol has rarely closed in on 100 units a year. So where did it go wrong for us?

The British car empire was formed in around 1924, when the country's largest car distributor, the Rootes family, started to acquire small and middle-sized manufacturers. Before the war, its portfolio included Hillman, Singer, Sunbeam, Humber, Talbot, and a few others. The majority of takeovers had started as bicycle manufacturers around the turn of the century.

When it comes to mergers, Britain is notorious. Perhaps one of the most scandalous stories was the way Rolls-Royce acquired Bentley in 1931. When the famous sportscar maker succumbed to the financial depression of the late 1920s, Rolls-Royce bought the company, hiding behind a made-up name of the British Central Equitable Trust. Up until the unfortunate events of 1998, Bentley was hardly anything more than Rolls-Royce's sidekick.

The high point of Rootes' acquiring campaign was surely the successful takeover of Singer, where the young William Rootes had served as an apprentice. He spent more than 40 years expanding his empire, but it took just ten years for the giant enterprise to

MG – the overtly sporty ADO16. (Courtesy Stuart Knight)

Riley Kestrel – the dignified but sporty ADO16. (Courtesy Stuart Knight)

be ruined by the 'emperor' himself. Although it would be completely wrong to belittle Rootes' input, there came a time when he started to struggle to keep up with the ever-increasing challenges and new trends of the car industry. He is known to have been part of the delegation travelling to Germany to give an expert verdict in the Volkswagen Beetle case. After the war, British forces controlled Volkswagen, and if British

Vanden Plas Princess – the 'posh' ADO16. (Courtesy Phil Seed)

businessmen had shown any interest in the defunct German company, they'd have had a chance to pack up all their assembly lines and know-how and sail back to Britain. When asked what he thought about the Beetle (that was eventually destined to become one of the world's best selling and most loved cars), he replied that the car was certainly too small and ugly for anyone to consider producing it. The official verdict of the delegation was: "To build the car commercially would be a completely uneconomic enterprise." A person lacking business intuition to such an extent as this was unlikely to drive the British car industry into a new era.

When, in 1963, Chrysler started its well-armed campaign to conquer the European car market, the Rootes company had few 'weapons' to help it fight the battle. Initially, Chrysler took over the French company Talbot, and then gradually increased control over the Rootes group. Sir William Rootes didn't live to see the demise of his enterprise. He died in 1964, and it was his son William Rootes II who succumbed to American pressure. It wasn't only due to bad management – one of the last independent cars developed under the roof of Rootes was the Hillman Imp. This was quite an innovative car, meant to advance the company in the changing scene of British motoring.

Unfortunately, the '60s marked the beginning of a series of unpopular decisions by the British government. It had recently introduced the principle of 'Industrial Development Certificates,' whose purpose was to bring industries to regions with a high rate of unemployment. Rootes had to build the Imp factory in Linwood, a small town in Renfrewshire, Scotland. People had never seen heavy industry there and, although they tried their best, lack of experience meant that, instead of securing Rootes' future, the Hillman Imp became one of the reasons for the company's demise. Besides, the parts and assemblies had to travel up and down the country from the Midlands to Scotland, which further dented the narrow profit margin. The Imp never really took off, and the poor build quality meant further losses for Rootes.

By 1967, Chrysler had finished the takeover, and Rootes' original models were dropped, one by one. Chrysler's European campaign wasn't a success story –

NEW HUMBER SUPER SNIPE

S A L O O N · L I M O U S I N E · S T A T I O N W A G O N

The Humber Super Snipe of the late '50s was one of the flagships of the golden era of British car manufacturing. (Courtesy Phil Seed)

it struggled to keep the old-fashioned British and French giants afloat, and the invasion ended in 1978 when Peugeot bought everything that Chrysler had acquired ... for a symbolic one dollar! That might sound like a real bargain, but considering that all Chrysler's European factories worked at a loss, Peugeot soon realised that it had bitten off more than it could chew. Demolition work began – the wrecking ball came down on the Linwood factory, and by 2007 Peugeot had demolished or closed everything that had once formed the Rootes empire.

However, Rootes was not the only car giant in the United Kingdom. In 1952, the British Motor Corporation appeared as a result of a merger between Austin and Morris. Meanwhile, the maker of commercial vehicles, Leyland, had acquired the sporty Triumph Motor Company, but Jaguar (one of the only profitable British car businesses of the '60s) bought the oldest British car manufacture Daimler. That is only the beginning of a string of obscure mergers that took place in the '60s. Soon, BMC joined forces with Jaguar to form British Motor Holdings, but it didn't help the situation – they joined and merged, completely forgetting about creating new models and working on publicity. In the end, encouraged by Harold Wilson's Labour government, the biggest merger took place. BMH merged with Leyland, which had now acquired Rover as well. The British Leyland Motor Company was born. This put an end to the mergers, and the opposite process of reorganisation began. In 1974, the huge, structure-less, and unmanageable company went bankrupt, and the government divided the monster into five parts. Due to the poor management skills of the executives, two of the parts had to be closed, while the remaining three – Rover, Jaguar and Land Rover – became a target for foreign investors.

The Rover P4, lovingly nicknamed 'Auntie.' (Courtesy Phil Seed)

The Rover SD1 was eagerly purchased in Europe. This is the Car of the Year logo in the Netherlands. (Courtesy Phil Seed)

The last truly British Rover was a real star. The new model SD1, better known as the Rover 3500, appeared in 1976. Its biggest selling point was the design. The SD1 is the very essence of English design – created from scratch by an in-house team. The car didn't copy any of the previous versions and offered a completely new way of looking at automotive evolution. Selling this new model was a risky enterprise – it meant closing and scrapping the well-oiled assembly line of the Rover P6, a neat but old-fashioned saloon. Should the SD1 face a fiasco, there would be no car to build. Luckily, the Rover SD1 was so unusual that the public soon fell in love with it. It also received acclaim from critics, although, as usual, there were some sarcastic remarks. In 1977, the new Rover won the 'Car of the Year' competition in Europe, receiving a total of 157 points – having edged 19 points away from the second generation Audi 100. Third place went to the Ford Fiesta – 1977 wasn't an easy yearin which to win the competition.

Even Audi's new engine didn't cut it – the expert international journalists presiding over the 'Car of the Year' jury chose the Rover, which had a veteran V8 – created in the early '60s – under the bonnet. Age didn't matter. Many will agree that the Rover V8 3.5-litre engine is one of the best in the world. With a dry weight below 380lb, it produced 158 to 190bhp, depending on specification. It lived on to power Land Rovers and TVR sportscars well into the 2000s. Today, it is still popular with kit-car makers, selling for anything from £1500 to £8000 (for the well restored and tuned 5-litre versions).

After the SD1, the real decline in the British car industry began. In the mid '70s, Vauxhall (although it lost its independence to General Motors in 1925) started producing exact rebadged replicas of the German Opel. Rover, lacking ideas and vision, formed a cross-holding with Honda in 1979, which eventually meant that there would be no more original Rover models. From then on, the entire range consisted of rebadged Hondas. In 1988, the government decided to start the privatisation of Rover, which was eventually acquired by British Aerospace.

British design at its finest – a beautiful Rover SD1. (Courtesy Michael Carpenter)

The last ever truly British Rolls-Royce – the Silver Spur. (Courtesy Rolls-Royce)

In the early '90s, due to huge financial problems and dropping share prices, British Aerospace decided to sell off all its non-aircraft businesses, including Rover. Thanks to BA management and Honda's experience, Rover went from an ailing giant into a profitable enterprise again. Its reasonably priced cars began to attract customers who otherwise would have bought a BMW or other import car.

Ironically, it was none other than BMW which bought Rover from British Aerospace for £1 billion. That proved to be a costly mistake. After pouring another £2 billion into the factory, BMW called it a day and, incredibly, sold Rover for just £10 in 2000 to a local consortium, Phoenix, led by John Towers, ex-Austin Rover Group director. His only wish was to keep the company alive and continue producing cars on a mass scale. His business plan required a £700 million investment. Half a billion pounds was provided by BMW just to get Rover off its hands, and the remainder came from the First Union Bank of North Carolina, USA. Towers established a new company, MG Rover Group, but, despite all his efforts, it went bankrupt in five short years. All equipment, inventory, and the MG badge was sold to the Nanjing Automobile Group of China, but the Rover badge, still owned by BMW, was sold to Ford. Despite the popular heritage of MG (Morris Garages), the Chinese have now come up with an alternative to this abbreviation: Modern Gentleman ...

The situation in the luxury car market was just as sad. In 1989, Ford acquired Jaguar. During its 20-year ownership, Ford hasn't earned a penny from Jaguar. Despite successful new models, the company was never profitable.

The real pride of Britain, Rolls-Royce, entered the turmoil in 1971. The company, which now produced aircraft and marine engines, as well as luxury cars, hit financial

Triumph 2000 and Rover P5 – two wonderful cars that had to suffer from unhealthy, in-house competition. (Courtesy Paul Brown released under Creative Commons licence)

difficulties and was split in two by the government. The aerospace counterpart was nationalised, while the motorcar division was sold on. In 1980, it was acquired by defence engineering company Vickers, which started showing an interest in the car business, consequently buying motorsport engineering company Cosworth in 1990. Once the initial enthusiasm had faded, Vickers decided to sell both Bentley and Rolls-Royce. Unfortunately, the government did nothing to stop it. As a result, our luxury marques continue successfully under Volkswagen and BMW respectively. Did you know that 7 per cent of cars sold worldwide are classified as luxury cars? This percentage fluctuates insignificantly and rarely drops, even during a recession. The luxury car market is a great sector to cater for, and losing the world's best luxury car marque was nothing less than a crime.

Most likely, the main problem of the British car industry was decentralisation and scattering of resources. Too much time and money was wasted on reorganisation and incorporation. Each of the British automotive mega-concerns had numerous brands and models that competed with other 'family' members. The consumers were confused because they didn't know which car to choose. For example, the factories making the Rover P5 and Triumph 2000 were owned by the same company. The cars appealed to the same niche – middle management and young professionals. The Triumph had to go and all the available resources had to be thrown in to honing the P5. Nevertheless, the bosses decided to stick with both cars.

The situation in the small family car sector was even more ridiculous. The Morris 1100, MG 1100, Vanden Plas Princess, Austin 1100, Wolsley 1100, and Riley Kestrel were the same car hiding behind different badges, restyled grilles and slightly different levels of interior finish. Although acceptable in the '30s, so-called badge engineering, started by Sir William Rootes, proved too much for modern, swinging Britain.

It certainly would have been possible to fight off the surge of Japanese and German cars if the British makers had concentrated on one model per sector. The resources that went into the restyling and rebadging of British cars would have been better used for a more concentrated publicity campaign, better engines, and brand-new models. Besides, the British car industry was faced with far too much uncontrollable industrial action, and not enough protection from the government.

In 2002, BBC journalists asked the question "Is the UK car industry in trouble?" and came to the conclusion that "… reports of the industry's demise are exaggerated." They didn't know that in just five years, there would be no car industry in the UK whatsoever. So, the question now is: are we ever going to get it back?

UNDER THE RED SEAL

There were many talented designers and constructors in the USSR who wanted to build beautiful and reliable cars. However, the leaders of the Communist Party mostly endorsed the production of rather unattractive cars.

One of the biggest successes of Russian designers was considered to be the Pobeda. Most of the pre- and postwar cars of the USSR were copies of popular, foreign cars. One would not want to mention this out loud, but everybody knew it to be the case. For example, the GAZ A was a close copy of the Ford A. However, it was a licensed copy, and Ford Motors knew about its Russian cousin's existence. The government's limo ZIS-110 was copied from the Packard 180, the Moskvitch 400 from the Opel Kadett K38, and the Chaika was reminiscent of the Packard Carribean. The record-holder in this discipline was the ZAZ-968, which combined the best and worst features of cars like the NSU Prinz, Chevrolet Corvair, Simca 1000 and Renault 8.

The Pobeda is often accused of plagiarism as well. This car is strikingly similar to the English Standard Vanguard. There are some historical facts that suggest this might just be a coincidence. The work on the Pobeda began in the late '30s. Because of the war, the engineers didn't have the chance to resume work until 1943. Three designers – Brodsky, Samoilov and Dolmatovsky – worked on this project, one after another. The revolutionary idea of a pontoon type body came from Brodsky. The only two people advocating the dropping of protruding wings and running-board was our good friend Gabriel Voisin, who conceptualised this new design strategy in 1935, and the Italian design studio Pininfarina, who created the Lancia Aprilia. You may notice similar features between the Aprilia and the Pobeda, but the Russian designers smoothed out the body features even further, and did justice to the pontoon style. The Pobeda made its debut in 1946, but about a year later, the Standard Vanguard appeared in England. There are no records to show that the English and Russian designers ever met. If it wasn't a case of industrial espionage, the similarity of the two cars must just have been a coincidence. Who knows? The front of both cars may remind you slightly of the prewar American cars. The compact size was dictated by the war, and smoothing out the features might have been the influence of Voisin. After considering those facts, the coincidence theory seems plausible.

The next few years offered little opportunity for Russian car design to develop, although there was potential to build on the phenomenal success of the Pobeda. The Soviet designers were distinguished by an extraordinary sense of shape, and they had the potential to bring a fresh breath of air into the world of car design. Yet the Party couldn't look beyond its principles, and all aspirations of the designers to improve the aesthetic quality of Soviet cars were similar to them banging their heads against a brick wall ... or, should I say, an Iron Curtain.

One of the most innovative concept cars built in the USSR was the NAMI 013 (at the NAMI Institute of Scientific Research in Automobiles and Motors). In 1953, Yuri Dolmatovsky began working on a streamlined car body. He tested various scale

NAMI 013 – an early drawing shows sophisticated design details that were not realised in the actual prototype. (Courtesy NAMI.ru)

Prototype NAMI 013 – the world's first 'cab forward' car. (Courtesy NAMI)

models of his brain-child inside an aerodynamic tunnel and got excellent results. The engine was placed at the rear, but the six-seater interior was moved forward. The front part of the cabin was outside the wheelbase. This type of layout offered more space for passengers. It was similar to the 'cab-forward' principle developed by Chrysler in the early '90s.

The head of the Institute thought that the NAMI 013 was very strange and a step too far from Communist ideals, so the project was stopped.

The Soviet leader, Nikita Khruschev, was of the opinion that the ideal car should be small and efficient. He gave relevant instructions to designers. Dolmatovsky, along with

NAMI Belka – a downsized and simplified version of the 013. (Courtesy NAMI)

Belka – a funny little car. Is this a rear view? Yes, it is. (Courtesy NAMI)

his colleague Ariamov, continued working on a streamlined body idea. They resized the NAMI 013 and changed it according to the orders of the Party. The four-seater concept car Belka (which means Squirrel in Russian), equipped with a motorcycle engine, met all of Khruschev's requirements, but the leader had lost any interest in cars, and Dolmatovsky's work proved futile once again.

VNIITE PT – a prototype of an urban taxi well ahead of its time. Some English engineers thought highly of this ultra-modern car. (Courtesy VNIITE.ru)

In 1961, VNIITE (the Scientific Research Institute of Russian Technical Aesthetics) was founded. Designers began to look more courageously into the future. It really seemed that stagnation would disappear at last, and the Soviet Union, too, would begin producing original cars. All the preconditions for it to happen were there – talented designers, Party 'blessing,' and an endless source of finance that the institute could spend to its heart's content. Besides, all raw materials could be sourced locally, and quite a significant number of car factories were capable of making almost anything. VNIITE designers created various interesting concept cars that didn't survive – the majority of them went for scrappage.

Part of the Dolmatovsky team's plan was to build a minivan, a small and ergonomic car for disabled people, a six-seater taxi, and even a sports coupé. None of the projects made it past the Party censorship. Soviet people seemed condemned to drive cars that were out-of-date, and sometimes rather ugly.

Designers lost heart completely when the AZLK C1 concept car was rejected. The C1, created in 1975, would replace the utterly outdated Moskvitch 2140. If Russian designers had realised the project, they would have surprised their foreign colleagues. The C1's appearance still looks fresh, even in the 21st century. Still, the managerial mob of Moskvitch rather took a fancy to the French Simca 1307, and decided to crib the new version of the French model.

After the collapse of the USSR, the designers at last had free rein, and were liberated from censorship's choking embrace. Some designers broke loose because there was no Party to answer to. During the first years of the newly founded Russia, the design studios largely specialised in tuning Ladas (the most popular cars in the former Soviet territory). It became very popular to try and improve the appearance of those basic cars by adding plastic spoilers and other funky features.

Amazingly, both research institutes (NAMI and VNIITE) survived into the capitalist era and continue working and generating ideas, despite scant finances. Many designers waited for the right moment and emigrated to work abroad. Some talented people decided to stay, regardless of the chaos, and continued polishing the traditions of Russian design.

One of the most recognised, independent car enterprises in Russia is CARDI, formed by students of the State Technical University of Moscow (MAMI). The director of the company, Sergey Alyshev, proclaimed his brainchild as the only real car design studio in Russia. He was once allegedly heard saying that CARDI was the first and

CARDI Body – the first concept car of Sergey Alishev. (Courtesy CARDI.ru)

The interior shows the lavish approach of Russian style. (Courtesy CARDI)

best design studio, and that it had almost no competition. This is not far from truth. At the time of writing, CARDI is acclaimed worldwide as the most professional car styling company in Russia.

Many foreigners who visit the Russian car shows find it hard to believe that CARDI's creations are built in Russia. Indeed they are – CARDI is just a group of Russian lads who have built on the knowledge and experience they gained at MAMI building great concept cars. The company employs less than 30 people and half of these are designers. The name CARDI is derived from an abbreviation of 'car design.' It is more of an art workshop than a car producer. Car prototype building is not a profitable business in Russia; that's why, apart from doing what it likes, CARDI also has to do something that pays, and tuning and customising foreign cars is still popular with Russian businessmen.

The company was founded in 1991, and, although it was clear that it wanted to build cars, in the beginning, the company produced something quite unusual for a car design studio – watches. It began building cars by relying on the sheer enthusiasm of the workers, and it actually took little time for the young designers to receive the acclaim they deserved.

Everything has to be perfect: even the engine compartment is an eye-pleaser. (Courtesy CARDI)

Their first successful show-car is probably one of the most extraordinary cars in all of Russian history. The CARDI Body made its debut in 1995, and quickly found itself to be the centre of attention. The retro-styled roadster was finished in high quality, and it was almost incredible that these young designers could have such an excellent debut. The roadster was quite small – only 3.6m long and 1.1m high, with a clearance of 5 inches. The technical capabilities of the car somewhat disappointed, but considering that the makers didn't have a decent budget for their first project, it was still a good result. The car was equipped with a conventional Niva (that's a compact Russian SUV) engine, producing just 90bhp and allowing the car to reach just 90mph. Still, the idea wasn't to break

CARDI Next with the targa top. (Courtesy CARDI)

An improvement on the previous SUV project – the hardtop Terra. (Courtesy CARDI)

the speed records. It was actually meant to be a fully functional concept car, and an example to other designers who often just presented a full-size model of a car.

Encouraged by the roaring success of the Body, the company rolled up its sleeves and began the next project – a lightweight two-seater holiday SUV. Niva was taken as the basis again – quite logically this time. The body was crafted in high-tech composite materials. The car was named 'Next,' and it was finished in just a year, hitting the 1996 Moscow car show.

Although the Next was a very cute car, the targa body type with removable roof panels was not really suitable for Russian winters. That's why the evolution model 'Tetra' was created – this time with a proper hard-top.

The model of 1998, the Curara, was CARDI's first international success. It made an appearance at the centenary Paris Motor Show, and is probably the most accomplished

concept car ever made by CARDI. Powered by a V12 BMW, and enhanced with an in-house sport suspension, this car was not only beautiful, it also had excellent dynamic, ergonomic, and handling properties.

The Body II captured near Vasilyevskiy Spusk in Moscow. The car is known to have been produced in small numbers. (Courtesy CARDI)

The atelier's last car in the series of original concepts was the Body II. It was finished in 2003 and went into small-scale production. It was built on the base of a BMW 3, and had kept the Bavarian engine, but the majority of technical solutions were created by CARDI. If somebody had developed the Body II into a large-scale project, it could have competed successfully with other giants of the fun-car sector like the Porsche Boxster and Mercedes SLK. It's even possible that many people would have found the Body II more appealing than the aforementioned roadsters.

Body II – a Russian design wonder against the background of a Russian architectural wonder, the 1555 Saint Basil's Cathedral, Moscow. The Kremlin is on the left. (Courtesy CARDI)

Curara – an aggressive and handsome car that could compete with any European fun car contender. (Courtesy CARDI)

Until now, apart from a heavy-duty military 4x4 concept, CARDI has concentrated on high-class car tuning and industrial design. The car industry in Russia is currently going through a hiatus, and to think about new prototypes or production models would be more than reckless. The Body II will remain – for the connoisseurs – one of the best car designs Russia has produced, but the most poignant moment of the company's history is the deal with the famous petroleum company Yukos Oil. CARDI created a design for the motor-oil bottles that the petrol magnate was preparing to sell. Because of the Yukos scandal, after its founder Mikhail Khodorkovsky was jailed, the beautiful green motor-oil bottles were sold in limited quantities. Now the green lump of plastic is considered a desirable object for collectors. Yukos memorabilia is in high demand.

Sergey Alyshev, world-renowned car designer, with a life-size model of Fortis amphibian. (Courtesy CARDI)

Meanwhile, CARDI continues to concentrate on industrial design projects and car tuning. Its latest project is a truly amazing vehicle called Fortis. It is an 'aerosani' amphibian, driven by a powerful propeller. Fortis can travel on water, bog, snow, or ice. More concept cars, or even a small-scale production, are possibilities. The company is known to be fulfilling orders of copies of its previous concept cars and all sorts of non-standard vehicles.

CARDI's most recognized tuning effort is the Monomah project. At first it looks just like a Maybach limousine, but it is much smaller. What's the catch? It turns out that the Monomah is a Mercedes E-class that has been transformed into a Maybach clone by the skilful designers. The company works with rich clients, helping them to add a personal touch to their car. It has created special accessory sets for cars like Hummer, Lexus, Bentley, and Land Rover, because owners of these cars come to the design studio most often. However, CARDI is not only about rich people – it is possible to order a sleek set of accessories for democratic cars as well.

After almost twenty years, the designers at CARDI have become world class

Amphibian Fortis feels confident where other means of transport don't dare to go. (Courtesy CARDI)

Although Fortis has been designed for a Spartan ride, the cockpit is surprisingly comfy. (Courtesy CARDI)

A Mercedes E-class cleverly disguised to resemble a Maybach limo.
(Courtesy CARDI)

Volga GAZ-3111 – this typical example of Russian car styling was a head turner, but failed to sell. (AvtoGAZ Publicity image)

professionals, and it is rather unfortunate that they still have to build furniture and other industrial design objects in order to keep their car design studio afloat. Although there is no Communist Party to interfere with the efforts of Russian designers, it is not exactly the most profitable time of their lives.

The future of the large car factories in Russia is uncertain. It seems that, just like Great Britain, they are losing the battle to keep their automotive traditions alive under the pressure of the foreign car-maker surge. From the three gigantic passenger car manufacturers of the Soviet era, VAZ (Lada), Moskvitch, and GAZ, only the former is going strong. Moskvitch went bankrupt in 2007, and GAZ, despite introducing several new models recently, only produces passenger cars sporadically. However, kept afloat by its commercial vehicles division, GAZ will most likely strike back, providing even more opportunities for Russian designers to express their creativity.

PART THREE

THERE IS NOTHING NEW ABOUT A CAR

THE GREATEST INVENTIONS IN MOTORING HISTORY

1673: internal combustion engine

Gottlieb Daimler is often cited as the inventor of the internal combustion engine. Nicholaus Otto is another name associated with this wonderful invention. Both gentlemen did a great job to make the engine what it is today, but neither is the actual inventor. We mustn't forget about the men who worked on the incredible horseless carriage concept 200 years before Daimler.

The first man who suggested the possibility of replacing a horse with something more suitable was Leonardo da Vinci, whom we can easily consider him the ideological godfather of the engine. Although da Vinci never mentioned generating mechanical energy from heat, he outlined the philosophical basis and introduced the idea to future generations to look deeper.

Christiaan Huygens – the guru Dutchman is considered the godfather of the internal combustion engine. (Public domain image)

The French inventor Abbe Hautefeuille, and Dutch physicist and astronomer Christiaan Huygens, continued the famous Italian thinker's work on a more practical level. Towards the end of the 17th century – more than 150 years after da Vinci's death – they began investigating, independently of each other, the idea of a single cylinder combustion engine.

It was probably the cannon that inspired the scientists. The heavy artillery weapon is considered a prototype of the modern internal combustion engine. The gun barrel was changed into a cylinder, and the cannonball was changed into a piston; and so the fierce weapon of destruction became one of mankind's grandest inventions.

In the first experiments with the engine, specially treated gunpowder was used as fuel, as there was no petrol at that time. Experts doubt if Hautefeuille ever succeeded in building a functioning engine, but an absolutely established fact is that Huygens did. He even proudly demonstrated his invention to Colbert, the French minister of finance. Of course, in those times, Huygens lacked mechanical knowledge, and didn't have the technical capabilities to make his engine effective or to derive any decent power from it. Moreover, his engine functioned in a very unstable manner, and it stalled after a few revolutions. Huygens tried unsuccessfully to solve the problems with valves. You could hardly call them valves – they were just leather pipes attached to the inlet and exhaust. Still, considering the period they lived in, we can safely conclude that Hautefeuille and Huygens were the geniuses of their era.

Over the next one hundred years, nobody was able to repeat the duo's achievements. Not until 31 October 1791, when an English inventor, John Barber, improved the construction of Huygens and took out the patent for a combustion engine. Three years later, his compatriot Robert Street patented his original engine construction. Both Englishmen were only theoreticians, and occupied themselves with mechanics out of pure enjoyment. Neither of them thought of mounting the engine onto a carriage and sending the horses to have a good rest.

Nicéphore Niépce, although known as the inventor of photography, built one of the first working prototypes of an internal combustion engine, helped by his brother. (Public domain image)

A schematic reconstruction of the cart built by Francois de Rivaz. (Public domain image)

One of the first working prototypes of an engine was built by the Niépce brothers in France. In 1807, they took out a patent for an engine that they named a 'pyreolophore.' The same year, the Swiss inventor François Isaac de Rivaz offered his version of the internal combustion engine. De Rivaz, unlike Huygens with his peaceful cannon, used gas as a fuel – it was a mixture of hydrogen and oxygen. In 1813 he built a car – it was 6 metres long and weighed more than a tonne. You couldn't get very far with a vehicle like that.

In 1824, Nicolas Carnot cemented a strong theoretical basis for future engine developers,

Etienne Lenoir built a horseless carriage that could cover significant distances. (Public domain image)

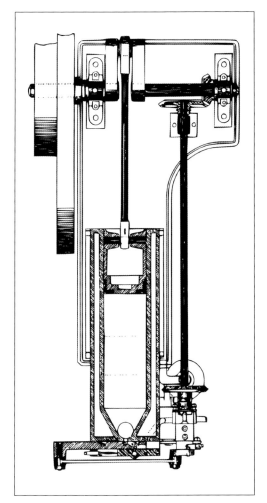

Illustration from the documentation for a patent granted to Nikolaus Otto in 1877. (Public domain image)

by describing the theory and thermodynamics of a heat engine. At the end of 1860, Etienne Lenoir, a Belgian engineer, came quite close to success. He equipped his so-called Hippomobile with a two-stroke single cylinder hydrogen engine. He derived the gas from hydrolysis. In 1863, Lenoir, driving his vehicle, covered 11 miles from Paris to Joinville-le-Pont within three hours. His engine produced a 'huge' output – half a horsepower. Still, it proved to be enough to manage 11 miles without breakage.

Lenoir is also considered the first car engineer to succeed commercially. By 1865, more than 500 of Lenoir's engines functioned in Paris. Some were used to power vehicles, but the majority of them were installed in pumping stations. It is interesting that the first engine prototypes were hugely different from the engines of our time – for example, the compression camera was separate from the cylinder.

In 1867, another scientist joined the game. German inventor Nicholaus Otto possibly had the biggest impact on the development of engines. He owned a small grocery shop in Cologne. Maybe he would have stood behind the counter until his old age, if he hadn't been inspired by a book that described one of de Rivaz's inventions. After that, Otto couldn't imagine himself as a shopkeeper any more. He closed the shop to make space for a workshop, and built a new, four-stroke internal combustion engine. It was the first time somebody had managed to put theory into practice. Otto's engine was working swiftly and there was enough power. Now he just had to put it on a carriage and drive.

The principle of how a four-stroke engine functions is now called the Otto cycle, but history has almost forgotten the man who was the first to describe it – Alphonse Beau de Rochas. He designed an engine with a compression camera on top of a cylinder – just like in modern engines. However, Rochas was careless, and Otto managed to take out the patent before the Frenchman.

Only then, after 200 years of trial and error, was it Gottlieb Daimler's turn to improve the construction of his predecessors. He did a great job, and solved many problems. He built proper valves and gaskets, and by 1885 had learnt how to build industrially viable engines. However, he is not the inventor of the internal combustion engine.

1834: electric cars

Although Honda, General Motors and other car giants have been playing with experimental electric car prototypes for decades, none of them is considered the inventor of the electric car. Today, when this idea finally seems to be taking off, many people think of electric cars as something new and recently invented. In fact, electric cars are much older than petrol cars, with a history spanning back more than 170 years.

In 1834, Thomas Davenport, an uneducated blacksmith from Vermont, USA, built a car with a small electric engine. Although the idea of transforming electrical energy into mechanical was pioneered by Britons Michael Faraday and William Sturgeon, it was Mr Davenport who first saw the potential, and used an electric motor to power a device. After a few years, independently from Davenport, Scotsman Robert Davidson became interested in electric motion, and built an electric locomotive that was considered too expensive to run. His compatriot Robert Anderson built a usable little electric cart that could actually be driven, but the biggest failing of both men's vehicles was the limitation of the feeding system. Rechargeable batteries weren't available in those days, amd therefore every time a battery was used up driving the vehicle around, it had to be discarded and a new one installed.

A new stage of development in electric car history began in 1859, when French physicist Gaston Plante invented the lead-acid battery – the first rechargeable one. Camille Alphonse Faure, another Frenchman and acclaimed chemical engineer, significantly improved the design of the lead battery in 1881. Although the resources were there, until 1888 no-one ever dared to think about building electric cars for public use. Fred Kimball from Boston eventually built an electric car that could do up to 15 miles between recharges. It was a noteworthy achievement. Even if the speed of this car was just 5mph, fellow Bostoners regarded Kimball's car as an important symbol of the town. Initially, it seemed possible that Kimball's design would go into mass production, but due to unknown circumstances it never happened.

Although the history of electric car development is rather fragmented, it seems that it was in Britain that large-scale electric vehicle production started. In 1888, Moritz Immisch, an Anglo German engineer, and Radcliff Ward both founded transport companies in London. Immisch attempted to make electrical trams and small cars, while Ward Electrical produced electric omnibuses for the city. Neither of the enterprises was very successful, though.

Around the same time in the USA, several small bicycle and engineering companies started to occasionally produce three-wheeled electric vehicles, but the real breakthrough came around the turn of the century. In 1898, Cleveland, USA, saw the rise of the first mass-production electrical vehicle company – Detroit Electric. Maybe if events had turned out differently, Cleveland might have become the capital of the American motor industry. Around 1905, Cleveland Electric built approximately 800 cars per year – almost twice as many as the Oldsmobile petrol cars.

In 1899, Camille Jenatzy forced the ever-sceptical Europe to look at electric cars from a new angle. He managed to set the land speed record in his torpedo-like electric car called Jamais Contente (which means 'never satisfied' in English). It is hard to imagine why Jenatzy was dissatisfied – he managed to squeeze 66mph out of his supercar. He later went on to experiment with the hybrid car idea by building one that had both an electric motor and a gas engine. That happened in around 1905 – so you can see how far back the hybrid car really goes.

Meanwhile, in the USA, a real electric car boom started. During the early years of the 20th century, there were 25 companies in the USA making electric cars, and the majority of New York taxis were electric. Not everyone believed in the future of motoring. The owners of Studebaker, the company that was destined to grow into one

National Electric Combination Vehicle. Style B. Price, $1,500, complete.

National Electric Run-About. Style A. Price, $3,000.

National Electric made practical cars for business and leisure. Part of a 1901 sales brochure. (Courtesy Charles Test, chuckstoyland.com)

of the best loved carmakers of the pre-WWII era, thought that motorcars would never take off. They continued concentrating on perfecting their horse carriages, but, driven by curiosity, they built an occasional bicycle, and finally, in 1902, an electric car. Later, they were converted to the idea of motoring.

One of the mightiest figures of the American electric car golden era was the Woods Motor Company. Its best years were from 1899 to 1918. The fact that Woods began its activities with a 10-million dollar start-up capital was the evidence of how firm its belief was in the future of electric cars. It was an unbelievable sum of money for that time. The electric cars' prices at the turn of the century fluctuated from $1000 to $3000. Woods was an innovative company, but what it is probably most famous for is introducing the electric car to the Hawaiian islands. Until 1902, Hawaiians didn't know about the existence of vehicles, and they welcomed the first electric cars with reverence and admiration. In 1915, Woods introduced a hybrid car with both electric and petrol motors.

Detroit Electric was another company producing a huge number of electric vehicles. Between 1907 and the late 1920s, it had assembled over 12,000 passenger vehicles. By 1912, it was selling almost 2000 cars a year. Although Detroit Electric models were quite heavy due to the battery packs, they could achieve a range of 80 miles on an advanced nickel-iron battery.

Modern day electric car critics place much emphasis on the fact that such cars have a low range. It is indeed one of the main problems plaguing their return. We haven't moved away significantly enough from what the early 20th century electric cars were capable of. The early production e-cars could cover 40 to 60 miles. Today it is 80 to 120 – not a giant leap by any means.

However, the sceptics at that time couldn't do anything about the fact that electric cars were far superior to any other means of transportation. A horse would need to stop every 10 or so miles for rest and water. Besides, a horse was slow, it kicked and bit, and it needed food. More and more people moved to towns, and horses somehow just didn't fit in. Steam carriages were difficult to use. It sometimes took more than 30 minutes of burning for the steam to form and the car to start. Petrol vehicles showed promise, but because of the lack of the automatic starter, they were unsuitable for women or anybody who was not extremely strong. Besides, the hand crank was dangerous, and many people were injured by it.

Most Americans believed that the electric car was the real solution for the growing transportation problem. That's why it came as a surprise to many to see electric cars disappearing from the streets of American towns as suddenly as they had appeared. Why did this great invention have such a short life – only a quarter of a century? There were three things that drove the nails into the e-car's coffin. One was Charles Kettering, who introduced an electric starter for petrol cars. That freed the people from the need to crank their cars, and made a petrol car more appealing.

The second was the sorry state of the road infrastructure of the USA. You might be wondering why the wheels of the first cars were so big. It certainly must have been hard for a gentleman wearing tight trousers or for a lady clad in a splendid long dress to clamber into the high vehicles. Although, to some extent, the diameter of a wheel was dictated by the unsatisfactory gear ratios in the early gearboxes, the main reason for keeping the wheels big was the roads. In America, as anywhere in the world at that time, good roads were few and far between. A modern car wouldn't go far in the Wild West. The rutted lines among the corn fields that turned into jolly brooks as the rain came couldn't be really called roads. The situation in the towns wasn't much better. Although some of the streets were cobbled, most were not – they were made up of gravel and soil. An electric car was often powerless in such conditions. Although it was frisky enough on a smooth surface, when it came to the delights of off-roading, its

Woods Electric targeted its advertising campaign at the fairer sex. Ladies loved the electric cars because they were easy to start. (Public domain image)

A National Electric car advertised alongside a gasoline/petrol car in 1909. (Courtesy Charles Test)

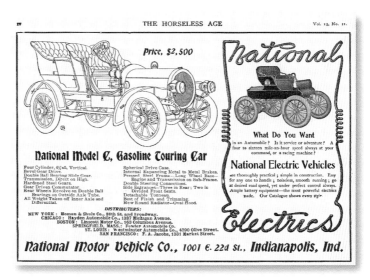

power just wasn't sufficient. Pushing or towing a car out of trouble wasn't easy either – early electric cars were heavy because they had to carry huge battery packs. For example, an average electric car concealed some 50-60 rechargeable batteries under its body, making some bigger models weigh as much as 2 tonnes. Batteries easily accounted for 40-50 per cent of a car's weight. A petrol car was lighter, it didn't stick in the mud quite so badly, and it had relatively more power.

Essentially, an electric car was suitable only for townspeople – electrification of rural regions began with President Roosevelt in the '30s. Farmers had to drive something, and they certainly couldn't join the electric car appreciation society. However, the townspeople also had problems with electricity. No unified voltage standards existed in the early 20th century. Seeing a wire, you couldn't really be sure what flowed through it – was it alternating current or direct current, and what voltage? It was like solving a riddle. The grid was unstable, and sometimes it was a challenge to recharge a car even if you lived in the posh part of town. The famous physicist Thomas Alva Edison advocated the use of direct current (of course he did – after all, his company distributed it!). His opinion was that direct current was the most handy form of electricity for the household. Westinghouse – the first American power supplier giant – didn't agree with him, and tried to persuade people to cut into the alternating current line. The electric car producers were perplexed – they couldn't build cars and charging devices that would suit both types of clients. All early electric cars used direct current, and eventually the manufacturers sold their cars kitted with a rectifier and a stabiliser, which was a big, unwieldy device and very expensive as well. It seemed strange that the standard equipment of an electric car included only the cable, and the customer had to buy the rectifier separately.

The final thing to put an end to electric vehicles was the economy. It may be cheaper today to drive an electric car, but back then, at the dawn of motoring, petrol was so cheap that no-one really worried about fuel consumption. Around 1915, an electric car still cost anywhere between $1500 to $2500. $2500 in 1910 is quivalent to around $50,000 in today's money. As petrol engine technology became more advanced, it was possible to buy a petrol car for as little as $500.

Everybody wanted to drive a car. However, only the richest townspeople could afford to plug into the power grid. In 1905, 1kWh of electricity cost 20-40 cents,

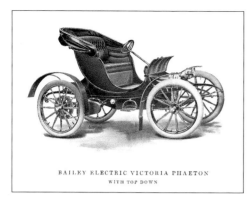

BAILEY ELECTRIC VICTORIA PHAETON
WITH TOP DOWN

Bailey Electric Victoria Phaeton – a nice little runner from a 1909 sales brochure. (Courtesy Charles Test)

Henney Kilowatt – the forefather of modern transistor-controlled electric cars. This one is known to reside in Austin, USA. (Courtesy Mark and Alyssa Farver, revoltcustomelectric.com)

depending on the provider, and 40 cents was a lot of money. One litre of petrol was just short of a cent. And if we are talking distances, a litre of petrol can get you much further than 1kWh of electricity. Today, it is quite a different story. People have learnt to produce energy very cheaply, and it is now up to five times more economical to drive an electric car than a petrol car.

By the 1930s, every electric car manufacturer was closed or had changed its profile. There had been attempts to reinvent the electric car. In 1959, Henney introduced the Kilowatt – a small, wacky car, based on the Renault Dauphine, incorporating modern technology not very different from that used in modern electric cars. Although around a thousand cars were produced, barely half of them were sold. The next chance for the electric car to strike back was in 1991 when, inspired by the fuel crisis of the previous decades, General Motors announced the debut of an electric concept car. It evolved into the famous (or infamous) General Motors EV1 car that went onto an experimental production line, and was tested by professionals and selected individuals. During the mid-'90s, several other companies like Honda, Peugeot and Ford made electric concepts for the sake of fashion, but it is not until now that we can really say that the electric car is coming back. Although it seems like an innovation, let's remember that the idea is actually almost two centuries old.

THE GREATEST INVENTIONS IN MOTORING HISTORY

1838: fuel cells

In 1967, General Motors announced that it would build the first car with a fuel cell system. Perhaps it was the first car, but it certainly wasn't the first vehicle to use fuel cells. The principle of this unique way of generating power was devised a long time ago.

Fuel cells, just like an ordinary battery, produce electricity via chemical reactions, but whereas a battery's chemicals are concealed within, the fuel cell itself doesn't contain any chemicals – the necessary chemicals are delivered from the outside. The process that takes place inside the cell is the very opposite to electrolysis – oxygen and hydrogen are turned into water, which is the only by-product of a fuel cell. So, there are no hazardous chemicals, which is why environmentalists love it so much.

William Grove was the first person to think about reverse electrolysis. The lawyer from Swansea in Wales was keen on chemistry and other natural sciences. To use electrolysis, it is necessary to consume electricity. So, maybe it would be possible to create an opposite process, where electricity is generated by combining oxygen and hydrogen? After many experiments, in 1839 he succeeded in creating a device that generated current from those widespread gases, with water as a by-product. He named his invention 'the gas battery.' Grove was a genius, but unfortunately he was born too early. At the beginning of the 19th century, it was hard to find a use for such an extraordinary appliance.

Steam engines and horse carriages dominated the world at the time, and the vast majority of people were convinced that the current order of things would carry on forever. The invention of William Grove proved unnecessary later too, because the internal combustion engine swiftly replaced steam. The first time anyone showed an interest in the magnificent Grove's gas battery was when American space engineers at NASA (National Aeronautics and Space Administration) were struggling to find a reliable source of energy in space in 1960. They were preparing for a manned mission into space, and a spaceship needed a steady source of secure electricity on board to make all the systems function. If they had to carry heavy lead accumulators with them, the spaceship would barely be able to take off. What about solar batteries? By 1960, the photovoltaic elements (solar batteries) were known and used, but they had several disadvantages – they were too big and produced too little electricity. To get anything out of solar batteries, they had to cover a huge square footage. Nuclear energy was another option looked at by NASA, but it soon abandoned the thought as it was too dangerous. Nobody could predict how a mobile nuclear power-station would behave in space.

Then somebody remembered William Grove and his gas battery. NASA used this brilliant old idea, and did a great job turning what was just a clever idea into a practical device. It was comparatively small, yet produced sufficient electricity, and many US spaceships have used the fuel cell system ever since. This is what the Americans named the new battery, and the name has stuck.

Soon afterwards, General Motors decided to reinterpret the idea of the fuel cell for civilian use. In 1967, it built a minivan prototype, called the Electrovan, that was powered by fuel cells. The vehicle was very heavy – it weighed 3.4 tonnes. With a filled hydrogen tank, it could cover 130 miles and reach a maximum speed of 62mph. Although GM's work showed potential, the Electrovan project was cancelled because it was impossible to resolve a few serious issues. The high weight and safety were the biggest concerns. Because hydrogen was needed to produce electricity, it had to be carried on-board in a pressurised container. It was potentially very dangerous as it could quite easily explode. However, during experiments involving fuel cell cars, there hasn't been a single explosion so far. With the introduction of new materials for the hydrogen containers, it is possible that the safety issue has been resolved. Unfortunately, the high cost of assembly makes it difficult to use fuel cells for mass-production vehicles. Less than ten years ago, it was announced by experts that if a fuel cell car went into production, its retail price would have to be more than $100,000.

At the beginning of 2005, General Motors carried out another experiment on fuel cell cars, delivering a few Chevrolet Silverado trucks to the US army. It was successfully tested in a non-combat environment in US military bases. The soldiers allegedly liked it, and asserted that it was as powerful as a 'real' V8 car. The range of the Silverado was limited to 80 miles, yet the car was powerful – its electric motor produced 180kW, which is only 20kW less than Silverado's petrol cousin.

During the last few years, it seems that the largest car manufacturers regard fuel cells as one possible way of driving automotive progress. Toyota and Daimler AG are both working on new fuel cell car models. The latter is planning to produce an experimental batch of 200 B-class fuel cell vehicles that could be leased to customers in Europe and the USA. Apparently, safety and cost are not issues any more; however, the infrastructure is still a problem. Although there are a few petrol stations in Germany and the USA offering hydrogen refuelling, the infrastructure is still too weak to support any significant number of hydrogen cars. However, many companies are working to solve this problem. The Commonwealth Scientific and Industrial Research Organisation in Australia has built a prototype of a hydrogen home station that could theoretically produce pure hydrogen from water electrolysis, by harnessing electricity from solar batteries. If it succeeds, we could all afford to install a hydrogen refuelling station at home in the near future.

1860: supercharger

One could not really imagine a performance car or any tuned car without a supercharger or a turbocharger. Increasing the volume of air to further increase burning (the burning of fuel in the car's case) is an age-old idea. Maybe we should thank an ancient Egyptian blacksmith who invented the bellows?

It was brothers Francis and Philander Roots who built the first supercharger for industrial devices in 1860, although they couldn't imagine that their invention would be used to power horseless carriages 40 years later. They built the blower to supply coal miners with air, having dug very deep under the earth in a search for a better coal-bed, whereupon breathing had become difficult. Roots' blower was huge and heavy, it was powered by a steam engine, and made largely of wood. Soon, they discovered that a similar device could be used to increase the efficiency of a metallurgical furnace.

When Gottlieb Daimler read about the Roots brothers' supercharger, he decided to build something similar, only much smaller. So, in 1900 a Daimler car became the first 'charged' vehicle in the world. In 1902, Renault and several others offered a charger as an optional extra on their automobiles. Although it really increased the power, customers weren't that impressed because it drove the car prices up. For example, American Chadwick built a car that could reach 60mph – an unbelievable speed for the early 20th century – but it was very expensive, so people weren't too keen on it. A model with an atmospheric engine cost $1000, but one with a blower cost $1400.

A supercharger wasn't ideal for cars, though. It was powered by a crankshaft, therefore the engine had to waste mechanical energy in order to increase the oxygen. A turbocharger, which is an air compressor powered by exhaust gases instead of a crankshaft, was built by Swiss inventor Alfred Büchi in 1905, but it wasn't until 1920 that his turbochargers appeared on ship engines. In the early '60s, American car makers finally began equipping the new breed of muscle cars with turbochargers.

THE GREATEST INVENTIONS IN MOTORING HISTORY

1893: carburettor

The prototype of the modern carburettor was invented by Hungarian mechanical engineer Donat Banki in 1893, in collaboration with fellow engineer Janos Csonka. German engineer Wilhelm Maybach submitted his patent half a year later. It is unknown if he had heard about Banki's invention or just thought of the same idea independently. Two years later, Maybach and Gottlieb Daimler combined their efforts to improve the fuel delivery system even further, and Banki joined in in 1898, by inventing a dual carburettor (with two barrels). The main construction of a carburettor remained almost unaltered for more than 100 years. Although the vast majority of cars are now produced with a fuel injection system, there are companies that continue to build carburettor engines.

So, what about the horseless carriages that operated before Maybach, Daimler, and Banki? How were they fuelled? In 1875, German-born Austrian engineer Siegfried Samuel Marcus created a brush-type atomiser. Marcus' invention was a small fuel reservoir with a round brush immersed inside. The brush was joined to a crankshaft and revolved quickly, which stirred up a small whirlwind inside the reservoir. Microscopic drops of fuel were taken off the surface and the air stream carried them into the engine. But Marcus' carburettor wasn't perfect. It wasn't possible to adjust the combustible mixture; it was either too lean or too rich, and, most of the time, a black cloud of smoke curled out from the car's exhaust.

English engineer Frederick William Lanchester built his first wick carburettor in around 1890. It was a revolutionary construction that vaporised the fuel from a series of wicks immersed in petrol. It took a while to improve the device and he did not file for a patent until 1905. It was by no means perfect, even though it was better than the Marcus carburettor. It consisted of two main compartments. The lower compartment held the fuel in which the wicks were immersed. They stretched towards the upper compartment where the air flowed through and picked up the vapour. Lanchester's carburettor produced an incredibly lean combustible mixture; nevertheless, his car worked fairly well. Moreover, for the first time in history, this fuel system was equipped with a coarse filter – a wire-mesh strainer that kept out impurities. No-one before Frederick Lanchester had thought to filter the fuel. It was only later that an external fuel

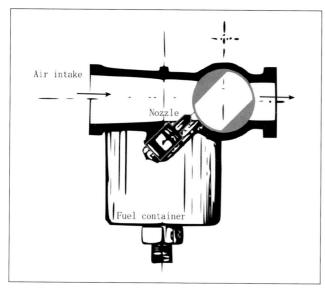

filter was advertised. The driver had to put a wisp of wool inside the funnel before filling his car. A proper air filter on top of a carburettor (as it is now in all modern cars) did not appear until 1915, pioneered by Packard on its Twin Six models.

An early, English-made carburettor. The air passing through the duct picks up microscopic drops and vapour of petrol from the nozzle.
(Public domain image)

1901: disc brakes

The first car brakes were rather archaic. They mainly consisted of a block fastened to a long lever, operated from the driver's seat. The driver had to use his own power on this device to apply the brakes to an axle or tyre. With such unsatisfactory braking, even a car that couldn't exceed speeds of 10mph sometimes rolled on for dozens of yards before it came to a halt. For this very reason, it is incomprehensible why the car producers used log brakes and drum brakes for so long, when the more efficient disc brakes were almost as old as the automobile itself. Still, as with every new invention, they were plagued by problems, and it took decades to bring the concept to perfection.

Two gentlemen fought for the honour of being the inventor of disc brakes. The most likely version is that Englishman Frederick Lanchester invented disc brakes in 1901, although the records show that he had been working on them since the mid '90s. Americans, however, assert that the real inventor was Elmer Ambrose Sperry, who used disc brakes on his electric car in 1898. Lanchester was famous in Birmingham, and when he stopped his car, ladies ran away in horror and put their hands over their ears – the brake callipers were made of copper and screeched hellishly when applied. Also, the copper wore off quickly, making disc brakes quite expensive to replace. Lanchester's compatriot, Herbert Frood, managed to eliminate the noise in 1907 by lining the callipers with asbestos. He had founded his company, Ferodo, in 1897, and although he gained fame as a producer of armoured vests, he went on to produce different brake products. Today, although not owned by the British any more, Ferodo is still functioning and still making brakes.

The main question in the history of car brakes is why it took people half a century to adapt the disc brake idea for mass-produced cars! Although the first commercially-built passenger car with disc brakes was the Tucker Torpedo, it was actually in Europe that manufacturers first began equipping the front wheels of cars with disc brakes. Around the early 1950s, many luxury and sports car manufacturers began doing this, and the first to offer disc brakes was the 1953 Jaguar C-Type, with other British and French manufacturers following soon after. In America, despite an early Chrysler attempt to make the most of the more advanced braking mechanism, it wasn't until the mid '60s that disc brakes really took off.

Of course, proper brakes are a major factor in traffic safety. Although drum brakes are indeed less effective, many car manufacturers in India, China, South America and Eastern Europe have entered the 21st century with drum brakes. Progress has a bad habit of being seriously delayed in certain parts of the world ...

Englishman Herbert Frood improved the
concept of disc brakes.
(Copyright Federal Mogul Corporation)

1902: all-wheel drive

Modern off-road vehicles that conquer mud and sand with ease are not a novelty. Even the WWII American 4x4s aren't regarded as the pioneers of the full-wheel drive. It is Dutch engineer Jacobus Spijker whom we can thank for this invention.

At the beginning of the 20th century, Spyker was one of the most innovative car enterprises in Europe. It produced cars successfully, took part in motor races and was in demand by the rich. In 1902, Spijker made a car that was considered to be the first all-wheel drive in the world. This car had an extraordinary appearance, too modern for its time, and a 6-cylinder engine. In 1903, when the car made its debut, it was seen as absolutely incedible, because all the other competitors had equipped their cars with 4-cylinder engines. The Spyker was a 6-cylinder monster with a 8.8-litre displacement. It produced 60bhp, and reached a maximum speed of 47mph. Not only that, the Spyker could conquer any roads. The new Spyker was the biggest hit at the Paris Motor Show, and attracted a huge crowd of curious people.

Five years later, two brothers from Australia, Felix and Norman Caldwell, went even further than Spijker. They managed to build a four-wheel drive system that made all wheels steerable. This wonderful idea was used for lorries and agricultural machinery. Because the Caldwells lived down under, the world learnt about their invention rather late. The big car producers did not dare to revive the Caldwell idea until about one hundred years after they filed the patent for a system that transmits power equally to all four wheels of motor-driven vehicles. In 2005, Jeep built a concept car called the Jeep Hurricane – a really weird, four-wheel drive vehicle. It looked so innovative, which is why it is so strange to think that somebody else came up with this idea a century earlier!

The Spyker was a powerful beast with a huge 6-cylinder engine and all-wheel drive.
(Public domain image)

While we are on the subject of the four-wheel drive, Ferdinand Porsche deserves a mention. This genius German engineer created one of the world's strangest vehicles two years before Spijker. A 25-year old prodigy, Ferdinand made a light lorry according to the orders of the Austrian motor plant Lohner. They named the car Le Toujours Contente ('Forever Satisfied'). This was allegedly to mock Camille Jenatzy, who was never satisfied ('Jamais Contente') with his electric car. Although it was a remarkable car, it actually had nothing to do with what we now regard as a mechanical, all-wheel drive vehicle. Each wheel had a separate electric motor that got power from a petrol engine, which then generated electricity. Doesn't that sound like a really alien idea? It is hard to imagine how a young man at the dawn of motoring could come up with something like this.

Even modern engineers will agree that the all-wheel drive is one of the most difficult parts of a car. Porsche created a system that was really simple – it didn't need any mechanical transmission at all, and synchronising the electric motors was enough because each wheel had a separate source of power. The waste of energy was minimal, and the car was really efficient. For this reason, Ferdinand Porsche unknowingly became the godfather of hybrid vehicles. Today, engineers are considering building electric cars that would have a separate small electric engine for each wheel, and I am convinced that this idea will finally break through as commercially viable.

1903: windshield wipers

Although the general perception is that it is usually men who become inventors, there are many great inventions made by women. One of these women was a sharp-eyed and courageous lady who invented windshield wipers. It seems so simple and commonplace these days, but at the very beginning of the era of motorisation, nobody could imagine a way to do something about the rain and snow that fell against the windshield.

Everyone considered precipitation a natural and inevitable part of life. If you really had to drive in the rain, you'd need to stop constantly, get out of the car, and wipe the windshield with your hand to see at least a couple of yards in front of you. The lazier drivers used to just stick their arm out and flick the raindrops off. The arm, of course, would become wet, but, alas, it was all part of a driver's hard work.

In late 1903, Mary Anderson had to travel from Alabama to New York, and it was raining cats and dogs. She had seen cars and their moustached leather-clad drivers before, but it had never occurred to her how often the poor men would have to make stops in order to clean the windshield. The lady thought this was ridiculous, and an idea flashed through her mind. Reaching her destination, she took a sheet of paper and began sketching something. When the idea was put on paper, she took it to the patent office.

The young woman who hardly understood anything about engineering had invented the windshield wiper.

Anderson's device consisted of a lever and a swinging arm with a rubber blade, which was powered manually from the interior. At that time, nobody could enhance her invention by adding an electric motor, because it was too hard to make one small enough. Anderson was granted a patent in 1905. Amazingly, there had been other inventors before her trying hard to invent windshield wipers. All the previous attempts had one thing in common – they didn't work. How did this young lady accomplish a task that so many men failed at? It is very simple and yet so clever. She invented a spring system that pressed the rubber blade to the windshield. Anderson's invention, with a little improvement (and obviously powered by electricity), is still used in modern cars. Nevertheless, many years went by before her creation got the acclaim it deserved.

THE GREATEST INVENTIONS IN MOTORING HISTORY

At first, her windshield wipers made everybody laugh. Narrow-minded people asserted that wipers were the most absurd invention of all time. Who would turn his attention away from the road to turn a lever? Surely it was better to try to peer your way through a window covered in snow and clamber out of the car every now and then than to wipe the windshield with your hand? However, as the number of motorists increased, so did the discontent about the lack of visibility. Finally, the same drivers who once laughed about Anderson now demanded from the manufacturers that cars should be equipped with windshield wipers. Some ten years after Anderson's difficult trip from Alabama to New York, the majority of new cars had her invention installed as a basic feature.

Four years later, another lady, Charlotte Bridgwood, decided to improve Anderson's wipers, because it was uncomfortable to drive and manhandle the lever at the same time. In 1917, Bridgwood patented her automatic Storm Windshield Cleaner.

Though Charlotte Bridgwood was a successful businesswoman, neither she nor her daughter – the silent screen star Florence Lawrence – were successful in selling Bridgwood's invention. After six years, automatic windshield wipers became a standard feature on Ford cars, but the motoring giant didn't mention Charlotte Bridgwood as having pioneered the idea. Led by Ford's example, all serious car manufacturers introduced wipers in the next few years. Florence followed in her mother's steps and invented the first turning and braking signals. They were mechanical – a set of signalling 'arms' attached to the rear fender that raised or lowered when the driver pushed a button. She never earned a penny from her inventions though, as they weren't patented. Although history has preserved the names of the lady inventors, unfortunately, they got neither recognition nor material gain.

Mary Anderson and Charlotte Bridgwood aren't the only representatives of the fairer sex to have contributed to the development of the car industry. In the 1930s, geologist Helen Blair Bartlett developed a new type of insulation for sparkplugs. However, you must admit that a female inventor is destined for a hard life. The first recorded American female inventor, Sybilla Masters, devised a new, handy corn-mill in 1712. However, during the 18th century, the idea prevailed that a woman's place was in the home with the children. Just because she was a woman, the patent had to be filed in with the name of her husband, Thomas Masters. The patent clearly stated, "founded by Sybilla, his wife."

The spring mechanism devised by Mary Anderson to keep the wiper pressed against the windshield is still used today, with only slight alterations. (Public domain image)

1907: the first petrol station
The term 'petrol station' is used in the United Kingdom. The USA and Canada mostly use the term 'gas station'. Where was the first petrol station built? The answer to this question cannot be agreed on by historians.

In 1907, John McLean, the sales manager at Standard Oil of California (now Chevron), built the world's first gas station in Seattle, although some people maintain that it was a Shell subsidiary of Shell Oil Co – Automobile Gasoline Co – that first offered a drive-through refuelling service in St Louis, Missouri in 1905. Before that, petrol was sold from general stores, livery stables and chemists, packed in wooden boxes containing two five-gallon cans. It sounds funny now, but until 1890, petrol was considered a waste by-product of the oil refineries. They used this 'worthless' stuff to heat the refinery and other premises.

1908: electric klaxon
At the beginning of the 20th century, most drivers used loud expletives to keep careless pedestrians at bay. Those who were more polite rang a small bell that could be pulled by pressing a pedal or jerking a rope. This was very inconvenient, as it diverted the driver's attention and could result in an accident.

Many car producers mounted pneumatic klaxons on their vehicles – a pretty, shiny metal horn with a manual rubber balloon that resembled an enema. Klaxons of this kind were mounted on cars up to the middle of the 20th century. Meanwhile, in the USA, the first electric signal appeared in 1908. The inventor's name hasn't survived, but it is known that only a handful of car makers used the electric klaxon. Electricity was obviously necessary to operate this signal, and that was a big problem for early cars.

Although in 1859 French physicist Gaston Plante had invented a lead battery – the prototype of the modern accumulator – it was too difficult to get this invention into production. At the beginning of the 20th century, the majority of cars were equipped with dry cell batteries. These discharged quickly and were very expensive. That is the main reason why it took so long for the electric klaxon to become popular.

1910: fuel injection system
The idea that fuel could be fed into an engine other than through a carburettor came from a team of American inventors; Herbert Adams, Eugene Adams and Fay Farwell. Their car factory, Adams Farwell, wasn't really successful, mainly due to the high prices of their cars. However, they were eager innovators, and, during the short existence of their company, pioneered several unusual technical solutions. They tested the first fuel injection system in 1910, shortly before going bust. Later, their findings were adapted for use on diesel engines, but fuel injectors on petrol engines remained a utopia for several decades.

After WWII, the technical principles of a fuel injection system were developed to the point that they could be safely used in mass production. Yet, the car producers had apparently become too attached to the old values – the carburettor – and didn't wish to change anything. It was only in the middle of the '80s that fuel injection systems found a widespread use.

The most important person involved in making the fuel injection system what it is today is Robert Bosch. He began working on improving the Adams Farwell system in 1922, but again concentrated on diesel engines. A few years later, Swedish engineer Jonas Hesselman tried to reinvent a fuel injection system for a petrol engine. Bosch had more success, and in 1952 the first production car using the Bosch fuel injection system rolled off the assembly line – the Borgward Goliath GP700. In 1955, the Mercedes Benz 300SL followed.

1912: the starter

It took a hard manual effort to start a car at the beginning of the 20th century. The driver had to put a hand crank into the driveshaft hole under the radiator and turn it with all his strength. If he managed it, the car would began to hum; otherwise it would remain stubbornly silent. And what if the engine stalled while driving and it was raining or snowing outside? He would have to get out of the car and restart the engine.

All this meant that the driver had to be not only able-bodied, but also patient. The invention of an electric starter was inspired by a man's death (he was not the first person to be killed by a hand crank). In 1908, a lady drove her pretty new Cadillac along a deserted road when the engine suddenly stalled. What a nuisance! The brave lady found the hand crank and got out to try to start the car. After a rather lame attempt, she understood that it was a waste of time. Fortunately, or unfortunately, another Cadillac went past driven by Byron Carter, a friend of the founder of Cadillac, Henry Leland. Being a gentleman, he stopped his car and offered his assistance to the lady. The car started after a few turns of the crank, but Carter had allowed a lapse of concentration that cost him his life – he had bent down too close to the car. The engine backfired and shot the crank out of the shaft hole. It hit Carter in the head, and as a result he suffered severe concussion and several fractures to the jawbone. It might seem unbelievable, but another two people connected with the Cadillac company – Ernest Sweet and William Foltz – happened to be nearby. Although the engineers rushed Carter to hospital, he died of gangrene a few weeks later.

Henry Leland was in despair. He promised that Cadillac wouldn't kill anybody else, and demanded that his subordinates invent an automatic starter. Many engineers before Ernest Sweet and William Foltz had attempted to devise a more handy starting system, but they hadn't succeeded in making the starter reliable and effective. Unfortunately, Sweet and Foltz couldn't get anywhere with their new mission either.

Leland got really angry and sought help from outside the Cadillac camp. The talented engineer Charles Franklin Kettering responded to his plea, and by 1912 he and his team had built a capable electric starter. It was a small electric engine that could work as a generator and produce a current, too. Through a cogwheel coupling and a clutch, it could be connected to a flywheel. Kettering's starter was fed by something similar to a modern day accumulator. Leland was very glad, but Cadillac was now just a division of General Motors. The managers of GM poured cold water on his enthusiasm straight away. Kettering's starter was regarded as not strong enough, and too capricious. They met in the middle – Cadillacs were now produced with electric starters, but still kitted with the dangerous hand crank as a backup. In 1912, of the 460 models that were exhibited in the New York car show, only 19 cars were equipped with an electric starter. The process of electrification happened rather slowly, but, in 1924, out of 119 models, only nine cars were without an electric starter. How many people were killed or injured because of the backfiring crank? No-one knows. Statistics have nothing to say about it, but cars with cranks were still produced after WWII.

1918: hydraulic brakes

At the beginning of the 20th century, brakes were operated by mechanical means. They were difficult to operate and rather ineffective. Still, nobody could imagine that another type of brake was possible. American inventor Malcolm Lougheed designed a hydraulic brake system in 1918, and soon it was used on the Duesenberg cars. They were among the fastest and best cars in the USA, and as speed increased, brothers Fred and August Duesenberg realsied that effective braking was a vital factor.

Lougheed's hydraulic brakes with minimal modifications are still used in the 21st century. Yet, strange as it might seem, other large car producers didn't hurry to change from archaic mechanical brakes to hydraulics. Ten years after their invention, Duesenberg was the only producer using the new type of brakes. A small step in the right direction happened at the beginning of the '30s when Chrysler, Auburn, and Plymouth also began using hydraulic brakes.

The last conservative camp capitulated in 1939, when Ford at last acknowledged that hydraulic brakes were superior, and began to equip its cars with them.

1920-1973: improvements to driver comfort

1920
American inventor and chief engineer of the Pierce Arrow Motor Car Company truck division, Francis W Davis, employed power steering for the first time because he realised how hard it was to steer heavy cars.

1926
Jean Albert Gregoire, in collaboration with Pierre Fenaille, introduced the Tracta system, in what is considered to be the first front-wheel drive car in the world that could actually function. The assertions that Citroën built the first front-wheel drive car in 1933 are untrue. Companies like Ford, Ruxton, and Gardner experimented with similar technology before Citroën, but it was Tracta that made the first working system.

The Tracta sportscar – the sophisticated front-wheel drive system is hidden in the metal box. (Courtesy David Saunders, released under Creative Commons licence)

A close-up of the Tracta's front-wheel drive. (Courtesy David Saunders, released under Creative Commons licence)

1928
Ferdinand Porsche, reverting to his old Lohner all-wheel drive idea, continued the tests with hybrid drive. Toyota did not pioneer hybrids.

1929
Paul V Galvin of Illinois began working on a car radio receiver. He and Edward Stewart founded a battery company that in 1930 introduced the world's first commercially viable car radio, named Motorola, derived from the words 'motor' and 'victrola' (a type of phonograph).

1938
The first electronic turning signals were introduced by Buick. However, the idea was pioneered by actress Florence Lawrence.

1939
Packard cars were equipped with air-conditioners.

1948
Daimler Benz replaced handle-operated windows with electric windows.

1966
A revolutionary car was made in Britain. It had jumped several decades with all of its advanced technology. The Jensen FF was the first mass-produced car equipped with four-wheel drive, disc brakes on all wheels, and ABS. The anti-lock braking system

One of the best and most innovative cars ever built – the Jensen FF. (Courtesy Michael Carpenter)

was introduced in 1929 by Gabriel Voisin, who designed the system for the aircraft industry. The FF was the brainchild of Harry Ferguson (the abbreviation FF stands for Ferguson Formula). He designed the all-wheel drive system so that the torque was divided between the back and front axles in a ratio of 67:33. The car had perfect road holding, whatever the weather. The FF was equipped with a 330bhp 6.3-litre Chrysler V8 engine, and could reach 130mph. In 1967, the Jensen FF was awarded 3rd place in the European Car of the Year competition in recognition of its extraordinary mechanical qualities, but unfortunately this car was doomed to failure. It was rather expensive – only a fraction cheaper than a Rolls-Royce limo. In four years, only 320 cars were produced, but Jensen cleared the way for the future 4x4 cars like Audi and Subaru, which eventually delivered the technology to the masses.

1973
Several manufacturers jumped on the idea of airbags. The Oldsmobile Tornado and a few Cadillac models were equipped with a driver's airbag as an extra option. In 1989, the USA adopted a standard law that stated all passenger cars must be equipped with an airbag. Since its introduction, this safety feature has saved more than 20,000 lives.

The Oldsmobile Tornado was the first mass-produced car equipped with an airbag.
(Public domain image)

INDEX

ALSO FROM VELOCE –

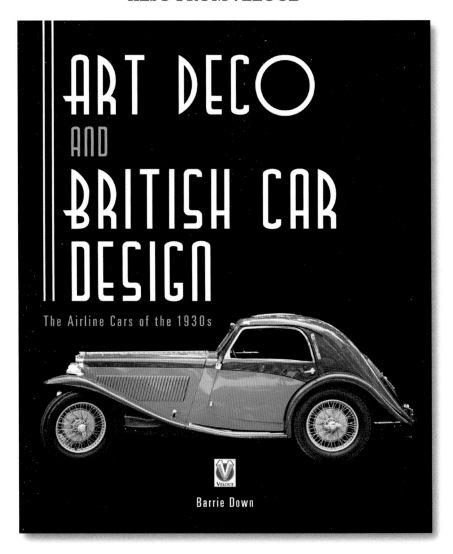

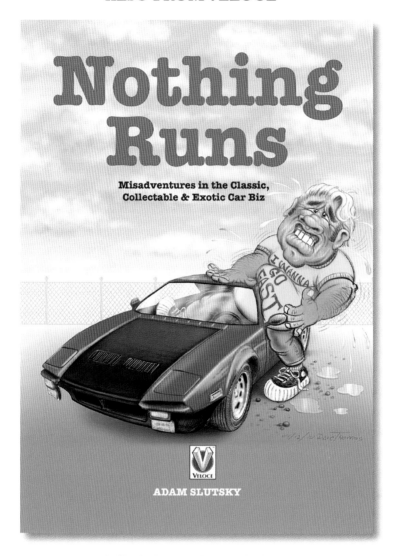

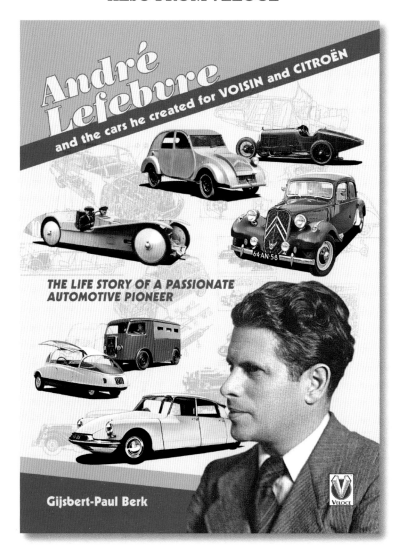